As one of the world's longest established and best-known travel brands, Thomas Cook are the experts in travel.

For more than 135 years our guidebooks have unlocked the secrets of destinations around the world, sharing with travellers a wealth of experience and a passion for travel.

Rely on Thomas Cook as your travelling companion on your next trip and benefit from our unique heritage.

Thomas Cook **pocket** guides

BERLIN

GW00598325

Your travelling companion since 1873

Thomas Cook

Written by Ryan Levitt
Updated by Cinnamon Nippard

Published by Thomas Cook Publishing
A division of Thomas Cook Tour Operations Limited
Company registration No: 3772199 England
The Thomas Cook Business Park, 9 Coningsby Road
Peterborough PE3 8SB, United Kingdom
Email: books@thomascook.com, Tel: +44 (0)1733 416477
www.thomascookpublishing.com

Produced by The Content Works Ltd
Aston Court, Kingsmead Business Park, Frederick Place
High Wycombe, Bucks HP11 1LA
www.thecontentworks.com

Series design based on an original concept by Studio 183 Limited

ISBN: 978-1 84848-307-1

First edition © 2006 Thomas Cook Publishing
This third edition © 2010 Thomas Cook Publishing
Text © Thomas Cook Publishing
Maps © Thomas Cook Publishing/PCGraphics (UK) Limited
Transport map © Communicarta Limited

Project Editor: Kelly Pipes
Production/DTP: Steven Collins

Printed and bound in Spain by GraphyCems

Cover photography (Murals, East Side Gallery) © FocusEurope/Alamy

CONTENTS

SYMBOLS KEY

The following symbols are used throughout this book:

ⓐ address 🕿 telephone Ⓦ website address 🕒 opening times
Ⓝ public transport connections ❶ important

The following symbols are used on the maps:

𝒊 information office		▣ points of interest	
✈ airport		○ city	
➕ hospital		○ large town	
🛡 police station		○ small town	
▣ bus station		═ motorway	
▤ railway station		─ main road	
Ⓤ U-Bahn		─ minor road	
Ⓢ S-Bahn		─ railway	
✝ cathedral			
❶ numbers denote featured cafés & restaurants			

Hotels and restaurants are graded by approximate price as follows:
£ budget price **££** mid-range price **£££** expensive

The following abbreviation is used for addresses:
Str.   Strasse (Street)

▶ *The Berliner Dom*

INTRODUCING
Berlin

Introduction

Rich history, fabulous art, alternative culture – in the broadest sense – combine to make the city of Berlin a holiday destination that is a little out of the ordinary.

The city's turbulent past and cosmopolitan citizens are its main draw; at every corner a piece of modern history plays out in front of you – whether it's the intrigue of the Cold War or the violent trauma of Nazism, it's all represented here.

But Berlin is more than just wars and destruction. Reunification in 1989 brought new hope to the German metropolis, and civic construction continues to boom. Visit this city once and you'll see some incredible views; return a few months later and the skyline will have changed considerably.

Always evolving, never stagnant, Berlin's residents have a laissez-faire attitude not found in any other city in the world. As the character Sally Bowles says in the quintessential Berlin film *Cabaret*, it's all about 'divine decadence'. Decadence is a double-edged trait, though, and it played a considerable part in ushering in the years of National Socialism under Adolf Hitler. While Berliners would ideally like you to forget this grim period in Germany's past, they won't deny its existence. Berlin was, though, actually the city at the heart of Communist support during Hitler's rise to power. During the crucial elections of 1933, it remained staunchly anti-Nazi – a fact that annoyed the Chancellor throughout much of his period in power.

A trip here offers something for everyone. Nature lovers adore the parks and rivers; fans of spy novels and thrillers can explore the streets chronicled in their favourite books; students of architecture can choose between classic buildings or modern structures; and fans of the arts will be overwhelmed by the volume of venues, galleries and museums. Better yet, head over to the Eastern neighbourhoods of Prenzlauer Berg or Freidrichshain, pull up a stool and sip beer with the locals who can tell you all about life in the former German Democratic Republic (GDR). You'll struggle to find a more fascinating holiday experience.

● Berlin – like the Reichstag – is a mix of the historic and the ultra-modern

When to go

Berlin is worth visiting at any time, since there is always plenty to do and see. For many, the city really comes alive in the summer. At this time of year one outdoor event follows the next, whether it is a colourful parade, street festival or an open-air concert.

SEASONS & CLIMATE

Berlin has a continental climate. In January and February the city often ices over, with spring thawing everything out some time in late March or early April. Summers can be hot and muggy but in early autumn and throughout spring temperatures are very mild, so this is a good time to explore the city's surroundings.

ANNUAL EVENTS

The tourist offices in Berlin (see page 153) can provide a full list of all the events in the city and surrounding areas. There's a comprehensive calendar at ⓦ www.berlin.de.

January

Berlin Fashion Week Fashionistas, supermodels and celebrities descend on the city. ⓦ www.fashion-week-berlin.com
Transmediale This cutting-edge festival for art and digital culture features exhibitions, live performances, lectures and workshops.
ⓦ www.transmediale.de

February

Berlinale Internationale Filmfestspiele Now 60 years old, the festival is one of the world's most important film events (see page 12)

March & April
Zeitfenster – Biennale Alter Musik The festival of ancient music is held on even-numbered years (2012, 2014) in the Konzerthaus (see page 75). Ⓦ www.zeitfenster.net

May
Karneval der Kulturen This multicultural festival is inspired by the Caribbean colour of the Notting Hill Carnival in London. Ⓦ www.karneval-berlin.de

🔺 *Karneval der Kulturen is a colourful celebration in Berlin streets*

Museumsinselfestival A four-month season of open-air rock and classical concerts kicks off on Museumsinsel (see page 40). Ⓦ www.museumsinselfestival.info

Theatertreffen Berlin The three-week drama fest offers the best in German-language productions. Performances tend to be innovative, provocative and extremely daring. Ⓦ www.berlinerfestspiele.de

June

Berlin Biennale This international contemporary art exhibition takes place on even-numbered years in various art spaces around the city. Events carry on until August. Ⓦ www.berlinbiennale.de

Berlin Philharmonie at the Waldbühne An open-air concert held during a single day in June (check website for details) in an atmospheric 'forest theatre' to mark the end of the Philharmonie season. Ⓦ www.berliner-philharmoniker.de

Christopher Street Day Parade The annual gay and lesbian pride parade is now one of Berlin's most flamboyant street parties. Gay and straight people take part in the festivities, usually held on the Saturday closest to 22 June. Ⓦ www.csd-berlin.de

Fête de la Musique On 21 June you'll hear music of all genres spilling out of every bar, café and music venue. Don't bother trying to have an early night – join in! Ⓦ www.lafetedelamusique.de

In Transit This international celebration of modern dance is held for three weeks every two years in early summer. Ⓦ www.hkw.de

August

Internationales Berliner Bierfestival This celebration of beer offers hundreds of brews from more than 60 countries. Ⓦ www.bierfestival-berlin.de

WHEN TO GO →

September & October
Art Forum Berlin An art trade show where over 120 galleries from many different countries present works. ⓦ www.art-forum-berlin.com

Popkomm An international music trade fair, conference and festival with plenty of great new acts. ⓦ www.popkomm.de

November & December
Weihnachtsmärkte Traditional Christmas markets spring up all over the city from the end of November up until 26 December. They're a great place to pick up unique last-minute Christmas gifts. ⓦ www.weihnachtsmarkt-deutschland.de

Silvester Berlin's New Year's Eve party – thousands take part in the celebrations at the Brandenburger Tor (Brandenburg Gate, see page 62). Expect a night of live music, DJs, food, drink and street partying galore. ⓦ www.silvester-berlin.de

---

PUBLIC HOLIDAYS
New Year's Day 1 Jan
Good Friday 22 Apr 2011, 6 Apr 2012, 29 Mar 2013
Easter Monday 25 Apr 2011, 9 Apr 2012, 1 Apr 2013
Labour Day 1 May
Ascension 2 June 2011, 17 May 2012, 9 May 2013
Whit Monday 13 June 2011, 28 May 2012, 20 May 2013
German Unity Day 3 Oct
Reformation Day 31 Oct
Christmas Day 25 Dec
St Stephen's Day 26 Dec

Berlinale Internationale Filmfestspiele

Berlin's International Film Festival, known as the Berlinale, takes place in February each year (for dates, check Ⓦ www.berlinale.de) and is a must for film-buffs. It hosts over 19,000 professionals from 120 countries and screens around 400 movies, the majority of which are world or European premieres. These are grouped under six categories: Competition (international), Panorama (independent/art-house), International Forum of New Cinema (experimental), Generation (films for young audiences), Perspektive Deutsches Kino (German films), and finally Retrospective and Homage, focusing on the life's work of a great cinema personality.

An international jury judges around twenty films which compete for the Golden Bear (Best Motion Picture and Lifetime Achievement) and the Silver Bear awards (Best Director, Best Actor and Best Actress). Previous recipients of Golden Bears include Patrice Chéreau for *Intimacy* and Michael Winterbottom for *In This World*. Winners of Silver Bears include Paul Thomas Anderson for his *There Will be Blood*, Benicio Del Toro for his role in *Traffic* and Kerry Fox for her performance in *Intimacy*. Running alongside the Berlinale is the international film trade fair, the European Film Market (EFM), and also the Berlinale Talent Campus. With an eye to the next generation, the Talent Campus invites 350 young film-makers from around the world to take part in a week of intensive workshops and discussions with professionals from the film industry. Some lectures are even open to the public: just check the programme and get yourself a ticket.

While the main Berlinale venues are at Potsdamer Platz, check the website for other locations around the city. From February you can browse the programme online and buy tickets. But remember if you do want to visit Berlin around Berlinale time, you'll need to book accommodation well in advance.

⬤ *Crowds gather for the International Film Festival*

History

Berlin was founded during the 12th century on an unpromising slice of swampland. Back then, nobody would have predicted this region would become a global capital.

The city came into prominence in 1416 when Friedrich of Hohenzollern defeated the Von Quitzow brothers to become the Elector of Brandenburg. This title allowed Friedrich to vote in the election of the Holy Roman Emperor – titular head of the German-speaking states.

Over the next three centuries, the economy heated up – and so did the Electors' ambitions. In 1701 Elector Friedrich III had himself crowned Prussian King Friedrich I, and a new empire was born. The Prussians were fervently militaristic, and consequently artistic life suffered. Every spare coin was pumped into the armed forces and the skilled labour required to support them.

When Friedrich II (Frederick the Great) assumed power in 1740, the nation was itching for a fight. Over the course of three years, Prussia snatched territory in Silesia in the East – the same region that prompted Hitler to attack Poland in September 1939.

Thanks to a natural abundance of raw materials, Berlin boomed during the Industrial Revolution, eventually leading to the fascist-versus-socialist splits that would divide the city a century later.

World War I was a nightmare for Berlin as the country's foreign and military policies were bungled at every opportunity. During the Weimar Republic that followed, Berliners became used to having to do such things as wheel barrows of money around the city to purchase a loaf of bread. This was because there were no manufactured goods to trade, so the government produced money by simply printing it. There was a plus side to Weimar, though, in the form of a devil-may-care permissive and free-wheeling social atmosphere. All of this ended abruptly when National Socialism (Nazism) reared its despicably ugly head in 1933, effectively bringing the Republic to an end.

As one of the few cities in Germany to reject Hitler and his policies, Berlin was a thorn in the Chancellor's side almost from day one. Hitler was determined to control the city, indeed he had to if he was to retain control of the country, yet he had little support within its borders. In order to quash opposition, he brutally cleared the capital of Jews, gypsies, homosexuals and Communists. Losses were, of course, enormous, and an incalculable amount of damage was done to Berliners' psychology.

When the war ended, the city was divided by the Allied forces. The Soviets were determined to get their hands on the tiny plot of capitalism that existed and closed off the city to the rest of the world in spring 1948. The Allies kept the city going by air-lifting food every 90 seconds into Tempelhof airport to feed the populace. After 11 months, the blockade was finally called off.

In August 1961, the city was divided for one last time with the construction of the Berlin Wall. The Wall remained until the collapse of the Soviet Union in November 1989, when the city – and the country – were reunified. What could have been a tortuous, and even fraught, process has been carried off with aplomb. Squatters who settled in East Berlin's abandoned houses started opening up music venues, independent cinemas, even soup kitchens, and Berlin soon developed an international reputation as the in-place for alternative music and culture. The city is still a little rough around the edges and in debt to the tune of €60 billion, but huge investment projects – such as the giant O_2 World indoor arena, which opened in 2008, and a huge 'Media Spree' urban development project – keep residents and visitors on their toes.

Lifestyle

Germany has a reputation for efficiency, sharp business minds, chilly receptions and a lack of humour. Anyone who believes this has never been to Berlin. The capital is the naughty kid brother to the other cities of Germany and its residents revel in this reputation.

Locals love a good time and have plenty of opportunities to indulge, though the economy isn't extraordinarily strong, causing most residents to budget wisely. This doesn't affect daily plans; instead it forces residents to think laterally. Admission costs to hip nightclubs are half what you would expect in other major cities and drink prices are affordable, meaning that even the most financially challenged souls can eke out a night on the town.

A typical evening out will start very late. Most clubs don't even open their doors until 23.00, and the funky and fashionable leave it another two hours before making their entrance. Bars are open (almost) all hours. Walk through most neighbourhoods and it is perfectly possible to find a bar open as late as 06.00. That doesn't mean Berliners are alcoholics; it just means they enjoy a leisurely drinking culture and the company of friends.

Although big business is growing in Berlin, with increased investment in many parts of the city, it has until now managed to resist being taken over by huge multinationals. A strong and individual community spirit survives as the city's biggest employers continue to be sole proprietorships and independent companies. When someone says they work for a family-owned company in Berlin, they really do – and the family will most likely have owned the company for many generations.

Shopping isn't the all-consuming religion that you'll find in Paris, London or New York. Hours reflect this: the bulk of shops remain shut on Sundays and have severely restricted hours on Saturdays – something that would be unheard of on London's Oxford Street. Instead, it's a beer and a gossip that residents like best, preferably at an outdoor café on a warm summer evening.

● *Enjoying a drink and a quiet chat at an outdoor café*

Culture

Berlin is a city in love with the arts. Public and private funding supports two major opera companies, a world-renowned philharmonic orchestra, countless chamber groups, experimental theatre troupes and dance practitioners – both classical and modern. There's also the annual Film Festival (see page 12), drawing a who's who crowd from Hollywood and the world of European cinema, and an incredible modern art scene that is widely considered to be one of the most influential in the world.

Berlin is remarkably celebrity-free, but with the Filmpark Babelsberg just outside of town and cheap studio recording space, there are always famous people stopping by. Recent regulars include Quentin Tarantino, Rufus Wainwright, Bloc Party, Joe Jackson and Peaches.

So why is Berlin so artistic? In many ways the Cold War is to be thanked. During the period of national division, West Berlin strove to become the most capitalist-friendly, glitz-filled, forward-thinking city in the world in order to act as a counterpoint to its dour Eastern counterpart. The theory was that East Berliners would be attracted by the glamour of an artistically vibrant West, and would battle the GDR-government to achieve freedom.

In many ways, this plan worked. While East Berliners were banned from watching Western television or listening to Western radio, many managed to do it. One of the first things Easterners did as soon as the Wall came down was to head to the legendary streets of Charlottenburg (see page 104), seen in so many programmes as the place where dreams could come true.

Other political decisions that helped to shape Berlin into an artistically focused city were the reduced taxes and national service waivers offered to youths who decided to live in the city. Berlin had

⬥ *The Altes Museum stages world-class exhibitions*

a desperate problem attracting residents – would you want to live in a city walled off from the rest of the world and subject to the threat of invasion at any moment?

In order to build up the population, German youngsters were offered the choice of performing mandatory military service for a year or moving to Berlin. As the peace movement and the arts often go hand in hand, the metropolis was flooded with artists who made a beeline for the vibrant district of Kreuzberg (see page 90). Squats sprouted up throughout the neighbourhood, and streets filled with music and art soon became commonplace.

Despite strong support for the arts, the sheer number of arts companies and organisations in Berlin is forcing a lot of rethinking. The glory days when the German government was dishing out ready cash to rebuild Berlin are well over, and locals are beginning to realise that there are simply too many world-class performers in relation to the size of the population. Moreover, Berlin's alternative culture is coming under threat from government crackdowns on squats and autonomous spaces, particularly along the river Spree. The Media Spree urban development project, which spans 180 hectares along the river and includes MTV Middle Europe and Universal Music Germany as well as the new 17,000-seater 02 World multi-purpose arena, is great for Berlin's economy – but does endanger its famously independent cultural scene.

As funding crises crop up more often, it is looking increasingly likely that some of the more niche companies will either be forced to close or move cities. So do Berlin a favour and drop a bit of spare cash in a donation box whenever you visit an arts institution. A single euro goes a long way.

▶ *View of Berlin from the TV tower*

MAKING THE MOST OF
Berlin

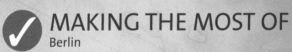

Shopping

Despite the fact that Berlin is a European capital, shopping options aren't all that stellar. Locals aren't known for their sense of style, with many limiting their purchases to the chain stores and bland ready-to-wear clothes found in the shops along Kurfürstendamm.

Better possibilities lie away from the main shopping drags in boutique-heavy residential districts. Local design work tends to be stylish, sleek and affordable when compared with similar products in Paris and London. Vintage shops around Hackescher Markt (see page 60) are well stocked with Adidas zip-ups, well-worn jeans, airline flight bags and chunky jumpers. German souvenirs are available in shops all over Berlin. However, most items associated with Germany are actually Bavarian, including cuckoo clocks and beer *steins* (tankards).

● *Take home a* stein *as a souvenir*

For keepsakes that are more Berlin-specific, wander over to **Mondos Arts** (ⓐ Schreinerstrasse 6 ❶ (030) 4201 0778 ⓦ www.mondosarts.de), where GDR-inspired goodies are available for purchase. Some of the more intriguing articles for sale feature the Ampelmännchen figure that's found on street signals throughout East Berlin. Designed to have more 'peasant-like' features, he is the jaunty man that signals

USEFUL SHOPPING PHRASES

What time do the shops open/close?
Um wieviel Uhr öffnen/schliessen die Geschäfte?
Oom veefeel oor erffnen/shleessen dee geshefter?

How much is this?
Wieviel kostet das?
Veefeel kostet das?

Can I try this on?
Kann ich das anprobieren?
Can ikh das anprobeeren?

My size is ...
Ich habe Grösse ...
Ikh haber grerser ...

I'll take this one, thank you
Ich nehme das, danke schön
Ikh neymer das, danker shern

Can you show me the one in the window/that one?
Zeigen Sie mir bitte das im Fenster/dieses da?
Tsyegen zee mere bitter dass im fenster/deezess da?

This is too large/too small/too expensive
Es ist zu groß/zu klein/zu teuer
Es ist tsu gross/tsu kline/tsu toyer

for you to walk or stop at most corners in Mitte, Prenzlauer Berg and Friedrichshain. Following reunification, there were moves to harmonise street signals in the city, but Eastern residents caused a huge uproar when told they might lose the little guy from their lives. When you cross the street, you'll realise why everyone thinks he's so cute.

Eating & drinking

Berlin has come a long way from the days when a *Bratwurst* and a pretzel were considered haute cuisine. Waves of Asian and Middle Eastern immigration and a long period of occupation by Western forces helped to change all that. Chefs are abandoning the standard pork-leg-and-two-veg dishes of yesteryear in favour of delicately spiced fusions.

Traditional restaurants remain popular and usually fall into two categories: tourist-oriented eateries featuring Bavarian chalet-style architecture and dirndl-clad servers, or hole-in-the-wall local establishments with hearty patrons and even heartier (and heavier) dishes. In either case, the meal is sure to be lip-smackingly good.

The sausage is so integrally part of German life that there are even sayings using the word *Wurst* to describe one's emotions. *Mir ist es alles Wurst* means 'It's all the same to me' or 'I don't care', but its literal meaning is 'It's all sausage to me'!

Berlin cuisine isn't the finest in Germany, but it is famous for drawing on the best the other parts of the country have to offer. The biggest contribution to *Wurst* culture is the decidedly Berlin creation of the *Currywurst*. Take one hot dog, grill it until cooked, sprinkle it with curry powder and lavish vast amounts of warm ketchup on it ... et voilà: Berlin's favourite fast-food delight.

PRICE CATEGORIES

Price ratings in this book are based on the average price of a main dish without drinks.

£ up to €12 ££ €12–25 £££ over €25

○ *Berlin's favourite fast-food*, Currywurst

If you're confused by the array of sausages on offer, a good way to remember the differences is that *Weisswurst* and other white sausages are milder in flavour and tend to come from Bavaria. Traditionally, they're only eaten in the morning or 'before the noon bells ring'. Heartier, spicier varieties, including *Bratwurst*, are eaten all day. And whatever you do, don't forget to put mustard on it or you'll be branded educationally bereft.

Pretzels are another Berlin speciality. New Yorkers may be a bit confused when they see them, however, as they won't be dusted with the thick layer of salt commonly found on most Fifth Avenue street corners. German pretzels are sweeter in flavour and softer in texture than your average American twisty. Served with beer, they make a nice change from peanuts and crisps.

Because of the poor growing conditions in surrounding fields, Berlin relies almost entirely on cabbage, potatoes and pork. Liver cooked with onions and apples is another speciality, albeit one that is hard to find in most restaurants.

Another tasty treat favoured by locals is the German noodle dish of *Spätzle*. A speciality of the region of Swabia, it consists of thick pasta, often topped off with cheeses, bacon and/or fried onions – possibly not a diet option.

Down your grub with copious *steins* (tankards) of beer. Berliner Pilsner is the usual brand of choice on tap at most bars and clubs. Keep an eye out for Berlin's annual Oktoberfest beer tent in the north of the city. It's not as famous as the one in Munich, but it'll quench your thirst for a good time.

Many of Berlin's most acclaimed restaurants serve international cuisine and are located in the wealthier neighbourhoods of Charlottenburg (see page 104) and Mitte (see page 60). Establishments in and around Friedrichstrasse are particularly chic and popular. Prenzlauer Berg and Friedrichshain (see page 76) also offer great culinary possibilities. That said, eateries will be more basic in look and feel. Luckily, the prices will reflect this lack of investment in swish interiors.

One interesting item to note is that the humble doner kebab was created not in Turkey but in the Turkish neighbourhood of Kreuzberg (see page 90). Stands are now scattered throughout the city, but for the true original make a beeline to the streets surrounding Görlitzer Park and the Türkischer Markt. Everyone has their favourite place to pick up these pita-wrapped meals, but the spicy treat truly comes into its own after dark when clubbers seek late-night sustenance following a long night on the town.

USEFUL DINING PHRASES

I would like a table for ... people
Ein Tisch für ... Personen, bitte
Ine teesh foor ... perzohnen, bitter

Waiter/waitress!	**The bill, please?**
Herr Ober/Fräu Kellnerin, bitte!	Die Rechnung, bitte!
Hair ohber/frow kelnehrin, bitter!	*Dee rekhnung, bitter!*

Could I have it well-cooked/medium/rare please?
Ich möchte es bitte durch/halb durch/englisch gebraten
Ikh merkhter es bitter doorkh/halb doorkh/eng-lish gebrarten

I am a vegetarian. Does this contain meat?
Ich bin Vegetarier/in (masc./fem.). Ist da Fleisch drin?
Ish bin veggetaareer/veggetaareerin. Isst dah flyshe drinn?

Where is the toilet (restroom) please?
Wo sind die Toiletten?
Voo zeent dee toletten?

I would like a cup of/two cups of/another coffee/tea, please
Eine Tasse/Zwei Tassen/Noch eine Tasse Kaffee/Tee, bitte
Iner tasser/tsvy tassen/nok iner tasser kafey/tey, bitter

I would like a beer/two beers, please
Ein Bier/Zwei Bier, bitte
Ine beer/tsvy beer, bitter

Entertainment & nightlife

When it comes to life after dark, Berlin is a city of serious contrasts. Known globally for its outstanding orchestras and opera companies, the German capital is also party central in the world of industrial, punk and dance music. One evening can see you listening to clarinets, and the next coming over all robotic to the electronic strains of the experimental German band Kraftwerk.

Berlin's individual neighbourhoods and the residents who call them home tend to dictate the types of activities a visitor might find there. Charlottenburg (see page 104), known to attract the upper-middle classes and fans of conservative values, is the location to go for a high-end meal at a high-end price. It is also the location of the Philharmonie (see page 118). Performances here are incomparable and are often highlights on the city's social calendar. Three decades ago, a visitor wouldn't have been caught dead in any other neighbourhood, but reunification has changed all that.

Mitte (see page 60) holds a variety of showcase venues originally built to entertain the royal court. The Staatsoper Unter den Linden (see page 75) is a good example of the district's artistic importance. Other entertainment contributions to Berlin's cultural life include Bertolt Brecht's Berliner Ensemble, the Komische Oper and the Konzerthaus (see page 75 for all three) – the latter used for intimate performances by chamber groups or up-and-coming soloists.

As the neighbourhood is extremely commercial, clubs and bars are concentrated in the more residential areas of the district located to the north and east near Hackescher Markt (see page 60). This buzzy collection of streets and shops is one of the liveliest places to enjoy dinner and dancing after dark. In summer months many of the cafés spill onto the street, allowing locals the opportunity to enjoy the warm nights. Mitte-goers are an extremely selective bunch, drawn by the latest in interiors, culinary styles and cocktail strengths. Many of the clubs have used GDR architecture to their advantage by incorporating Communist design leftovers into their final products. The results are often inspiring.

● *Konzerthaus hosts many chamber music events (see page 75)*

As Kreuzberg and Schöneberg (see page 90) are very residential, bars and clubs here are extremely welcoming. You'll invariably be greeted warmly at any of the venues in these neighbourhoods, making them great regions to explore if you're visiting Berlin on your own.

During the Cold War era, Kreuzberg was the district of choice for artists, students and squatters. Many of these residents remain and have built up a collection of venues that combine great atmosphere with colourful interiors. A large Turkish population gives some venues an oriental flair and here, the birthplace of the kebab, you can always find a late-night bite.

Schöneberg, meanwhile, houses the largest gay and lesbian ghetto in town, so expect some wild nights in the bars and clubs of its intimate streets. Dietrich, Bowie, Iggy Pop and Isherwood have all been inspired by the area.

Finally, we arrive at Prenzlauer Berg and Friedrichshain (see page 76). Now firmly in the spotlight as the neighbourhoods of choice for lovers of late-night activity, it wasn't always this way. Cheap rents have created a simultaneous population and artistic explosion in both communities. With large industrial spaces going for a song, club promoters are laughing their way to the bank. Here is where you will find the headquarters of industrial, dance, pop, hardcore, house, techno and punk. Venues can crop up and disappear overnight, so it is best to prowl through the area's music shops to keep abreast of what's hot.

Berlin operates a strict smoking ban in most public places, including restaurants, bars and nightclubs. The exceptions are establishments smaller than 75 sq m which do not serve food and do not admit anyone under 18. Check before lighting up.

● *Berlin offers a wide choice of nightlife*

Sport & relaxation

SPECTATOR SPORTS

Football is popular in Berlin and the city boasts the magnificent Olympia Stadion (see page 107) where the final of the 2006 World Cup was played. The local outfit is **Hertha BSC Berlin** (W www.herthabsc.de).

A state-of-the-art 17,000-seater multi-purpose indoor arena, **0₂ World** (① 01803 206 070 W www.o2world.de), opened in 2008 and hosts basketball, handball and ice hockey matches as well as big-name concerts.

PARTICIPATION SPORTS & RELAXATION

Water sports

The River Spree and the urban waterway network that connects with it provide great opportunities for water sports such as canoeing and kayaking. Maps and guides are available from a number of agencies that can take you through the city or beyond into the surrounding countryside. For tours of the western river and canal system, for both beginners and more advanced paddlers, contact **Der Bootsladen** (ⓐ Brandensteinweg 37, Spandau ① (030) 362 5685 W www.der-bootsladen.de ① 12.00–19.00 Tues–Fri, 09.00–19.00 Sat & Sun, mid-Mar–mid-Oct; 13.00–16.00 Fri, 10.00–16.00 Sat, mid-Oct–14 Mar Ⓝ Bus: M49).

Fitness centres

Gyms are dotted throughout the city, some offering day passes as well as longer contracts. Try **Fitness First Lifestyle Club** (ⓐ Schönhauser Allee 80 ① (030) 446 7370 ① 07.00–23.00 Mon & Wed, 09.00–23.00 Tues & Thur, 07.00–22.00 Fri, 09.00–21.00 Sat & Sun Ⓝ U-Bahn: Schönhauser Allee).

RELAXATION

Berlin is blessed with parks and large green open spaces throughout the city, including the magnificent Tiergarten (see page 107). Originally a hunting ground for the Prussian Electors, the park was opened to the general public in the 18th century. In summer, it positively buzzes with activity: joggers, picnickers, families, frisbee throwers and office workers basking in the sun. As the park is so large (167 hectares/ 413 acres), it is perfectly possible to wander off the paths into hidden, tree-covered corners that feel like something straight out of a fairy tale. In winter, you can even cross-country ski along its many trails.

Another winter option is to rent skates at the outdoor rinks at Alexanderplatz or in the **Sony Center** (ⓐ Kemperplatz 1 ⓦ www.sonycenter.de), where it is also possible to try your hand at curling from late November to early January.

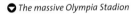
● *The massive Olympia Stadion*

Accommodation

The boom in development in Berlin is a bonus for travellers. Never before has there been so much choice. This has translated into great bargains as large properties do battle to fill their rooms. The exception to this rule occurs during the Film Festival (see page 12) and whenever there is a large-scale trade show in town.

Those who like their hotels with a bit more character won't be disappointed. Renovations, restorations and rebuilds have created new properties, including antique-packed salutes to art deco, sleek and chic boutique properties, and grande dame hotels featuring original GDR-period interiors.

Potsdamer Platz is the area to head for if gleaming glass and modern European hipness are your thing, while Mitte (see page 60) is 5-star, bells-and-whistles central. Alternatively, why not try a homestay or spend time in a smaller property in the residential district of Prenzlauer Berg (see page 76)?

HOTELS & GUEST HOUSES

Michelberger Hotel £ The hippest low-budget hotel in town, combining a trendy building-site aesthetic with sleek contemporary design and a grand piano in the bar. There are sometimes concerts in the courtyard. ❷ Warschauer Strasse 39/40 (Friedrichshain)

PRICE CATEGORIES

The ratings in this book are for one night for two people in a double room.

£ up to €80   ££ €80–140   £££ over €140

🔺 *Stylish and quirky design at Propellor Island City Lodge*

🕿 (030) 2977 8590 🌐 www.michelbergerhotel.com Ⓝ U-Bahn/ S-Bahn: Warschauer Strasse

Propellor Island City Lodge £–££ The quirkiest hotel in Berlin. Rooms are decorated by artist and owner Lars Strochen in a bizarre mix of styles: one is a peppermint green padded cell, another has everything completely upside down, and there are even matching white coffins in which you can, if you feel so inclined, sleep with the lid closed.

ⓐ Albrecht-Achilles-Strasse 58 (Charlottenburg & Tiergarten)
ⓣ (030) 891 9016 Ⓦ www.propeller-island.com Ⓝ U-Bahn: Adenauerplatz

Bleibtreu ££–£££ Darling of the media and fashion set, the Bleibtreu is a boutique property with a minimalist feel. ⓐ Bleibtreustrasse 31 (Charlottenburg & Tiergarten) ⓣ (030) 884 740 Ⓦ www.bleibtreu.com Ⓝ S-Bahn: Savignyplatz

Crowne Plaza Berlin City Centre ££–£££ Staff are friendly, facilities are top-notch (including a weights room, swimming pool and sauna) and the rooms are nicely designed in relaxing beige tones. ⓐ Nürnberger Str. 65 (Charlottenburg & Tiergarten) ⓣ (030) 210 070 Ⓦ www.cp-berlin.com Ⓝ U-Bahn: Wittenbergplatz

Hotel Art Nouveau ££–£££ Quality accommodation in a boutique-style hotel, with free Wi-Fi. ⓐ Leibnizstrasse 59 (Charlottenburg & Tiergarten) ⓣ (030) 327 7440 Ⓦ www.hotelartnouveau.de Ⓝ U-Bahn: Adenauerplatz

Hotel Garni Askanischer Hof ££–£££ Popular with theatre luvvies and literary folk, this little gem hasn't changed much since it opened in 1910. Furnished with antiques, it's got plenty of 'olde-worlde' charm and romance. ⓐ Kurfürstendamm 53 (Charlottenburg & Tiergarten) ⓣ (030) 881 8033 Ⓦ www.askanischer-hof.de Ⓝ U-Bahn: Uhlandstrasse

Park Inn Berlin-Alexanderplatz ££–£££ A massive skyscraper right on the Alexanderplatz, the Park Inn is a bit of a package-tourist destination property. So why stay here? The views. The Park Inn is one of the tallest buildings in Berlin and you can see for miles from the bedroom window.

🅐 Alexanderplatz 7 (Mitte) 🕿 (030) 23890 🌐 www.berlin.parkinn.de
🚇 U-Bahn/S-Bahn: Alexanderplatz

Casa Camper £££ In the heart of Mitte's designer shops and shoe stores, this stylish hotel adds a bit of zing to the Berlin hotel scene. 🅐 Weinmeisterstrasse 1 (Mitte) 🕿 (030) 2000 3410 🌐 www.casacamper.com 🕐 U-Bahn: Weinmeisterstrasse

🔺 *Top of the range accommodation at Hotel Adlon*

Hotel Adlon Kempinski £££ The ritziest hotel in town, the Adlon has been the address of choice for Berlin's elite since its opening in 1907. Staff can be a bit stuck up, and the rooms are a bit on the small side, but the address couldn't be more convenient. ⓐ Unter den Linden 77 (Mitte) ⓣ (030) 22610 ⓦ www.kempinski.com ⓝ U-Bahn/S-Bahn: Brandenburger Tor

Kempinski Hotel Bristol £££ The fanciest hotel on Kurfürstendamm offers the same fantastic levels of service as its Mitte-based competitors. Unfortunately, it lacks the history and graceful architecture. The exterior can remind guests of London's concrete South Bank. ⓐ Kurfürstendamm 27 (Charlottenburg & Tiergarten) ⓣ (030) 884 340 ⓦ www.kempinskiberlin.de ⓝ U-Bahn: Kurfürstendamm

Schlosshotel im Grünewald £££ Karl Lagerfeld designed every inch of this sprawling Schloss. While it is jaw-droppingly gorgeous, it's also inconveniently located unless you have a car. ⓐ Brahmsstrasse 10 (Charlottenburg & Tiergarten) ⓣ (030) 895 840 ⓦ www.schlosshotelberlin.com ⓝ S-Bahn: Grünewald

Westin Grand Hotel Berlin £££ An elegant hotel sitting gracefully on Friedrichstrasse. Look closely and you may still be able to see the tiny holes from recording devices planted by the GDR government to spy on some of the hotel's noted former guests. ⓐ Friedrichstrasse 158 (Mitte) ⓣ (030) 20270 ⓦ www.westin-grand.com ⓝ U-Bahn: Französische Strasse

HOSTELS
A&O Berlin Friedrichshain £ Clean hostel rooms featuring pine furniture and a cheery courtyard. If you're really into no-frills, choose

their 'just a bed' option. ⓐ Boxhagener Str. 73 (Prenzlauer Berg & Friedrichshain) ☏ (030) 8094 754 00 ⓦ www.aohostel.com ⓝ S-Bahn: Ostkreuz

Baxpax Downtown £ Conveniently located in Mitte, this hostel is clean, the staff are super-friendly and helpful with good tips for places to go and useful advice for easing into Berlin culture. ⓐ Ziegelstrasse 28 (Mitte) ☏ (030) 2787 4880 ⓦ www.baxpax.de ⓝ U-Bahn: Oranienburger Tor

The Circus £ The most popular hostel in town, Circus is a cheery and inexpensive oasis in the often dodgy world of rent-a-beds. ⓐ Weinbergsweg 1A (Mitte) ☏ (030) 2839 1433 ⓦ www.circus-berlin.de ⓝ U-Bahn: Rosenthaler Platz

Ostel Berlin – Das DDR Ostel £ If you're curious about the GDR (or DDR in German), then why not get your kitsch-fix outside a museum and experience its particular decoration first-hand? Choose from the 'holiday camp', the GDR apartment or Stasi Suite. Talk to the friendly staff about taking a spin in a Trabi (the GDR's automobile), hire a bike, or take advantage of the cheap breakfast. ⓐ Wriezener Karee (Prenzlauer Berg & Friedrichshain) ☏ (030) 2576 8660 ⓦ www.ostel.eu ⓝ S-Bahn: Ostbahnhof

CAMPSITES

Tentstation £ This is Berlin's only camping site. The nightly fee includes a shower, breakfast is cheap and if you're feeling energetic have a game of beach volleyball or table tennis. ⓐ Seydlitz Str. 6 (Charlottenburg & Tiergarten) ☏ (030) 3940 4650 ⓦ www.tentstation.de ⓛ 23 Apr–30 Sept ⓝ U-Bahn/S-Bahn: Hauptbahnhof

THE BEST OF BERLIN

Berlin is an ideal destination for a short weekend break because it is a city of neighbourhoods. Choose Mitte (see page 60) for history, Charlottenburg (see page 104) for shopping, Kreuzberg (see page 90) for community or Prenzlauer Berg (see page 76) for cutting edge.

TOP 10 ATTRACTIONS

- **Brandenburger Tor (Brandenburg Gate)** Once a symbol of power, now one of freedom and reunification (see page 62)

- **Museumsinsel (Island of Museums)** Explore the past at the Pergamon Museum, Alte Nationalgalerie, Altes Museum and stunningly restored Neues Museum (see pages 64–7)

- **Hackescher Markt (Hackescher Market)** Berlin's hottest complex of boutiques, galleries, bars and cafés. Go for the day or spend the entire weekend (see page 60)

- **Filmmuseum Berlin** You'll become a fan of German cinema after a visit to this amazing museum chronicling the history of the industry from *Metropolis* to *The Lives of Others* (see page 109)

⬇ *Charlottenburg Palace*

- **Reichstag (Parliament Buildings)** The German capital has been the epicentre of national events ever since the day it was built (see page 104)

- **Story of Berlin** Explore the history of the city in this well-executed museum that tells the story of Berlin through interactive stories and 3-D displays (see page 107)

- **Tiergarten** Considered one of the finest urban parks in Europe, if not the world (see page 107)

- **Jüdisches Museum** Daniel Liebskind's museum dedicated to the history of German-Jewish culture is a masterpiece. If you have time to visit just one museum, then choose this one (see page 94)

- **Haus am Checkpoint Charlie** The Wall may no longer remain, but the relevance of this museum dedicated to peace does. A fascinating journey through the Cold War period (see page 93)

- **Topographie des Terrors** The 'final solution' plan to destroy Europe's Jews was drawn up on this site. The original buildings have been replaced by a stunning new museum; the horror, however, remains (see page 93)

Suggested itineraries

HALF-DAY: BERLIN IN A HURRY

Stuck for time? Worry not. It's easy to see the bulk of Berlin's biggest sites in just a few hours. Start your day at the Reichstag (see page 104) and climb Sir Norman Foster's dome. From there, head to the Brandenburg Gate (see page 62) to see the symbol of reunification witnessed in so many news reports during the destruction of the Berlin Wall. Follow the Unter den Linden past Friedrichstrasse, stopping in any of the museums along the way, such as the **Deutsche Guggenheim** (ⓐ Unter den Linden 13/15 ❶ (030) 202 0930 ⓦ www.deutsche-guggenheim.de ❶ 10.00–20.00. Admission charge) or the Deutsches Historisches Museum (see page 65). End up at the Berliner Dom (see page 60) to savour the architectural splendour.

1 DAY: TIME TO SEE A LITTLE MORE

Begin your day at Potsdamer Platz to see how Berlin has grown over the past couple of decades. Step inside the Filmmuseum (see page 109) for a look at the masterpieces of German cinema, then follow Ebertstrasse up to the Brandenberg Gate (see page 62) and Reichstag (see page 104). Follow the Unter den Linden to the Museumsinsel for explorations of the four museums that call the island home (see pages 64–7), then hop along Bodestrasse towards Hackescher Markt (see page 60) for a relaxing coffee (or something a little stronger).

2–3 DAYS: TIME TO SEE MUCH MORE

With two or three days you can get a much better impression of what the city has to offer. Take the one-day tour recommended above. On day two, explore Charlottenburg (see page 104) – including shopping along Kurfürstendamm, plus trips to the museums and the sights surrounding Schloss Charlottenburg. On your final day, choose a walk around the up-and-coming neighbourhood of Prenzlauer Berg (see page 76) for a sense of 'real' Berlin. Alternatively, head down to Kreuzberg (see page 90) and visit the stunning Jüdisches Museum (see page 94) and Haus am Checkpoint Charlie (see page 93).

LONGER: ENJOYING BERLIN TO THE FULL

Get more out of Berlin by getting out of town. A visit to Potsdam (see page 122) will expose you to Prussian splendour, while Sachsenhausen (see page 120) provides grim reminders of the nation's Nazi past. Both will give you a fascinating glimpse into Germany's history.

● *Check out the modern architecture – and the shops – at Potsdamer Platz*

Something for nothing

Consider yourself prudent with the euros? Then you're in luck. Many of Berlin's most inspiring sights are absolutely free (or close to it). On warm days, one of the best Berlin experiences is a day in Tiergarten (see page 107). Sunbathe on the grassy lawns, or take a stroll along the paths. You might even spot a deer during your walk.

For inspiring views, head over to the Siegessäule (see page 106). Fans of director Wim Wenders' film *Wings of Desire* will immediately recognise the column from which viewpoint the angels used to watch over the citizens of Berlin. The structure was actually built to celebrate Prussian military victories. Climb the steps for just €2.20.

Continue east to enter the Reichstag – the German parliament buildings (see page 104). The Nazis took control of Germany in 1933 after they burnt the building down. Russian graffiti and bullet-holes can still be seen in the walls, left by the conquering military forces. It's free to enter and climb up into Sir Norman Foster's stunning glass dome, though you may have to queue. From here it's just a few steps south to see the Brandenburg Gate (see page 62) made famous as the backdrop to the reunification celebrations in 1989 when the Wall was dismantled.

Continue along Unter den Linden to the Deutsches Historisches Museum (see page 65). This museum chronicles the history of Germany and its relationship to the rest of Europe throughout the centuries.

If you time it right, you can even enjoy the museums of the Museumsinsel (see pages 64–7) free of charge. All the museums run by the state, such as the Altes Museum (see page 64) and the Pergamonmuseum (see page 67), are free for the last four hours every Thursday. A donation is appreciated but not necessary.

⬤ *Sir Norman Foster's amazing glass dome at the Reichstag*

Finally, one of the best things to do is simply to wander through Berlin's various neighbourhoods, each with its own distinctive flavour. Prenzlauer Berg (see page 76) remains fiercely socialist and artistic, while Charlottenburg (see page 104) is regal in tone. For a multicultural experience, head over to Kreuzberg (see page 90) or the Volkspark Friedrichshain (see page 80). Locals are very friendly, especially in the politically-aware Eastern neighbourhoods.

When it rains

As a city of museums and culture, you won't be at a loss if it ever starts to get a little wet. On inclement days, leave neighbourhood explorations to hardcore travellers and turn instead to the modern structures around Potsdamer Platz. There are plenty of things to distract you in the immediate area, including the Filmmuseum (see page 109), a massive shopping centre, and Berlin's largest cinema complex. If you can make a run for it, you can even dash over to the nearby Gemäldegalerie (see page 109) for an afternoon with the old masters or to the Neue Nationalgalerie (see page 110) for more modern works.

Another convenient location for keeping dry is the Museumsinsel, or Museum Island. The Berliner Dom (see page 60) and four major

⬥ *The stunning roof of the Sony Centre at Potsdamer Platz will keep the rain off*

COFFEE CULTURE

For a truly authentic experience, do as the locals do and enjoy a spot of café culture. Find yourself an inspiring place for refreshments, pick up a copy of one of the international papers and order a slice of apple strudel. The smell of slowly roasting coffee is sure to seduce and there's something incredibly romantic about watching the people of Berlin go by from the comfort of your warm café table. Berliners are famous for their adoration of coffee, so you won't be pressured to speed through your caffeine break, unless you happen to be sipping during a peak time. Go on a weekday when workers are busy behind their desks and you shouldn't have a problem.

museums are located on this island situated just off Unter den Linden. It's easy to pop between all five buildings if you're trying to kill time. Exhibits range from archaeological discoveries in the Pergamonmuseum (see page 67) to European art masterworks in the Alte Nationalgalerie (see page 64). The Altes Museum (see page 64) provides a space for temporary exhibitions, while the architecturally stunning Neues Museum (see page 67) displays prehistoric, classical and Egyptian antiquities. The Berliner Dom (see page 60) is an elegant church that was once attended by long-standing congregation members in two separate countries.

Trips outside Berlin aren't advised on bad weather days. Potsdam (see page 122) is too spread out to be enjoyed effectively in the rain. You'll simply get drenched if you try to manoeuvre your way between the various palaces. Sachsenhausen (see page 120), while atmospheric, is particularly awful, with large sections of the grounds turning into mud.

On arrival

TIME DIFFERENCE

German clocks follow Central European Time (CET). During Daylight Saving Time (end Mar–end Oct), the clocks are put forward one hour.

ARRIVING

By air

Brandenburg International Airport (❶ 1805 000186 ⓦ www.berlin-airport.de) is due to open at the end of 2011, around 20 km (14 miles) southeast of downtown Berlin. It is actually a major extension of the existing Schonefeld Airport (same details), the former airport of East Berlin. The new airport will have all the usual facilities, including shops, restaurants, ATM machines, bureaux de change and car hire offices.

Fast, regular S-Bahn and train services link Brandenburg and Schönefeld Airport to the centre and to other areas in the Berlin region. At Brandenburg, follow signs to the railway platforms directly below the terminal. At Schönefeld Airport, catch the free shuttle bus to the railway station. There are also plenty of taxis available, but be careful: this option will generally take longer and cost considerably more than the S-Bahn or train. It is a bad idea to take a taxi during rush hour, unless you are staying outside the city centre.

When Brandenburg International is fully up and running, Schönefeld Airport and **Tegel Airport** (❶ 1805 000186 ⓦ www.berlin-airport.de) will be closed. Tegel Airport is located just 8 km (5 miles) northwest of Mitte and has been, until 2011, the main airport for major national and international airlines. Frequent buses link Tegel Airport to various locations in the centre. Bus tickets cost €2.10 and are valid on U-Bahn and S-Bahn lines for two hours in one direction.

By rail

Berlin's mainline station, **Hauptbahnhof** (ⓐ Europaplatz 1
ⓘ (030) 2260 5805 Ⓦ www.hbf-berlin.de), is one of Europe's fastest, most efficient and most streamlined train stations. It is the main point of rail transport for the city to points east, west, north and south. Trains depart on average every 90 seconds, carrying hundreds of thousands of passengers every day. Inside the station you will find a shopping centre open 08.00–22.00 daily and plenty of cafés and eateries, as well as a left luggage facility (*Gepäckcenter*) on the first upper floor, open 06.00–22.00. Four providers offer wireless internet access within the station.

🔺 *Berlin's mainline railway station, Hauptbahnhof*

Hauptbahnhof is a major interchange on the S-Bahn system, serving lines S3, S5, S7 and S75 from the platforms upstairs. U-Bahn line U55 runs to Brandenburger Tor from its underground station. Several bus routes also pass by the station. Car hire desks are available on the first lower floor.

The station is fully accessible for disabled travellers, with lifts and hoists on the platforms and staff at the Mobility Service Centre on hand to assist. If you will need help boarding and alighting from a train, it's best to inform the station of your travel plans and needs at least one working day in advance.

By road

The arrival point for long-distance buses is outside the Zentraler Omnibus Bahnhof (ZOB) in western Berlin opposite the tall Funkturm, or Radio Tower.

Germany is an easy country to drive in, but remember that Germans drive on the right-hand side of the road. Streets are well marked and well lit, and the *Autobahn* (motorway) system is fast, efficient and extensive. From the cities of Western Europe, follow the E26 or E51 until you hit the city outskirts. From here, it is relatively easy to get into the centre by following the motorway signs. Parking is available both on-street and in protected lots. You may even qualify for free parking at your hotel. Consider selecting a more expensive hotel if you plan to bring your car and free parking is included, as daily parking rates can add up.

In 2008, Berlin, Cologne and Hanover introduced a new initiative to reduce pollution in inner-city areas. This means that if you're intending to drive your car to Berlin, you'll need to get its levels of emissions checked. Head to an authorised garage where you can pick up a permit sticker for €5. For more information in English,

IF YOU GET LOST, TRY ...

Excuse me, do you speak English?
Entschuldigen Sie, sprechen Sie Englisch?
Entshuldigen zee, shprekhen zee english?

Excuse me, is this the right way to the old town/the city centre/ the tourist office/ the station/the bus station?
Entschuldigung, geht es hier zur Altstadt/zur Stadtmitte/ zur Touristeninformation/zum Bahnhof/zum Busbahnhof?
Entshuldeegoong, gayt es here tsoor altshtat/tsoor shtatmitter/ zur Touristeninformation/tsoom baanhof/tsoom busbaanhof?

Can you point to it on my map?
Können Sie es mir bitte auf der Karte zeigen?
Kernen see es meer bitter owf der kaarte tsygen?

check the official website ⓦ www.berlin.de/umweltzone. If you're caught without a permit sticker you can be fined €40.

FINDING YOUR FEET
Berlin is a massive, sprawling city of individual neighbourhoods. When exploring specific districts, walking is often the best option. However, distances can be challenging for even the most hardened travellers.

ORIENTATION
Berlin is a city of wide avenues that cut through tree-lined residential districts. A ring road and ring-S-Bahn run around the city.

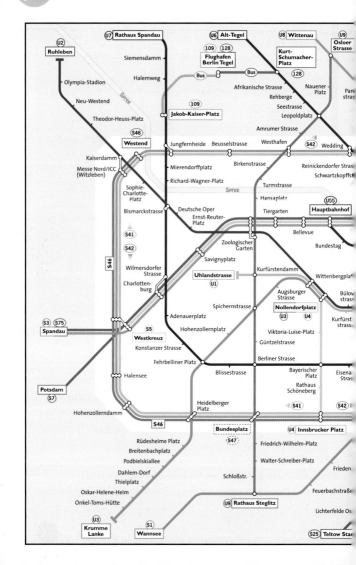

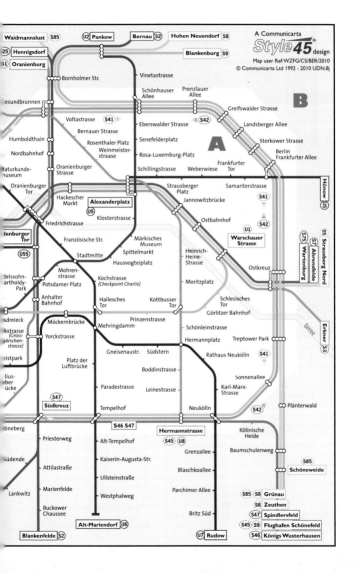

ß VERSUS SS

The German letter 'ß', called *scharfes S* (sharp S), is represented in English by 'ss'. For ease of use, all German names and words in this guide have been written using 'ss'. Be aware, however, that you may come across 'ß' when travelling in Germany; common uses include *Straße* (street) and *Grüße* (greetings).

To the west are Charlottenburg (see page 104) and the leafy park Tiergarten (see page 107). Charlottenburg has a suburban feel thanks to the shopping centres and chain stores that line Kurfürstendamm.

Kreuzberg and Schöneberg (see page 90) to the south are mainly residential. Both feature large ethnic minority populations and are well known for their pubs, clubs and markets. In the middle lies Mitte (see page 60) – home to the bulk of the major historical attractions and 5-star hotels. If you're looking for a museum, then chances are you'll find it here.

To the north and east lie Berlin's hottest neighbourhoods – Prenzlauer Berg and Friedrichshain (see page 76). These two former Communist areas feature large populations of artists and students attracted by the cheap rents and opportunities for gentrification. Friedrichshain, along with Kreuzberg, is where the alternative and activist subcultures are mostly based.

GETTING AROUND

With its extensive U-Bahn and S-Bahn networks and its multiple bus and tram routes, Berlin is an extremely easy city to get around. The city's transport website, Ⓦ www.bvg.de, has up-to-date information and a useful journey planner.

From Sunday to Thursday, U-Bahn and S-Bahn trains start running just after 04.00 and finish between 00.00 and 01.00. On Friday and Saturday most trains run through the night, with the exception of the U4 and U55.

Buses are handy if you're planning to paint the town red on a weeknight, when the trains do not run throughout the night. Trams (*Strassenbahnen*) are also handy, especially if navigating through East Berlin. Over 25 lines depart from the main terminus at Hackescher Markt (see page 60).

Tickets for all the listed methods of transport can be purchased from the ticket machines located in S-Bahn and U-Bahn stations. A single ticket, or *Einzelfahrausweis*, for Zone AB costs €2.10 and is valid for two hours (in one direction) on buses, trains and trams.

● *Nollendorfplatz underground station by night*

A *Tageskarte* (Day Pass) for Zone AB costs €6.10 for unlimited travel until 03.00. Don't forget to validate your ticket when boarding any method of transport. If you're unsure where the validating box is, ask another passenger.

If you're planning on staying a few days you might want to consider investing in either the 48-hour or 72-hour Welcome Card (€16.90 or €22.90 respectively for Zone AB), which gives you unlimited transport and also discounts on museums and tours. You can purchase them at one of the tourist information outlets that are dotted around the city (see page 153) or at the main railway station. Alternatively, buy them in advance via Ⓦ www.visitberlin.de.

CAR HIRE

Unless you are planning to drive out to Potsdam (see page 122), Leipzig (see page 134) or points further afield, you won't need to hire a car. While driving isn't a problem in this land of efficiency, the U-Bahn and S-Bahn system is, for most, just too extensive to warrant the expense. However, if you do decide to hire, some reputable companies are:

Avis ⓐ Schönefeld/Brandenburg Airport ⓣ (030) 6091 5710 Ⓦ www.avis.de

Europcar ⓐ Railway Station ⓣ (030) 2062 4600 Ⓦ www.europcar.com

Hertz ⓐ Schönefeld/Brandenburg Airport ⓣ (030) 6091 5730 Ⓦ www.hertz.com

The earlier you book your car, the better the rate – you can usually get good deals on the internet on booking websites such as Ⓦ www.mycarhire.co.uk. Note that age restrictions and/or extra charges apply at most companies.

◗ *The imposing Alte Nationalgalerie*

THE CITY OF
Berlin

Mitte

Mitte, literally meaning 'middle' or 'centre', is the heart of Berlin. The city's most important historical landmarks, most chic shops and most pricey real estate can all be found within this district's confines – and it continues to gain new buildings, memorials and attractions every day.

Most of the museums and sights in Mitte have finally been fully restored following the years of decline under the Communists. A memorial to the Jews who died in the Holocaust is a striking feature of the district: consisting of thousands of steles resembling stone pillars, it is located just south of the Pariser Platz.

The neighbourhood varies greatly depending on which corner you are exploring. The southern end feels very corporate, and is dotted with concrete skyscrapers, while a walk along the Unter den Linden will take you back in time to the days of the Kaiser. Finally, there is the residential and shopping quarter around the Hackescher Markt, which is well worth checking out for some truly original finds.

SIGHTS & ATTRACTIONS

Berliner Dom

Destroyed during World War II, the Berlin Cathedral has been fully restored. An Italian Renaissance masterpiece, it sat as a ruin from the end of the war until 1975, when the Communists finally decided to rebuild it. For years, the congregation was one of only a few that could boast long-standing members in two separate nations. Some West Berlin families remained staunchly loyal to the church that was separated from them by politics and concrete. The church continues to hold services for devout German Protestants. ⓐ Lustgarten

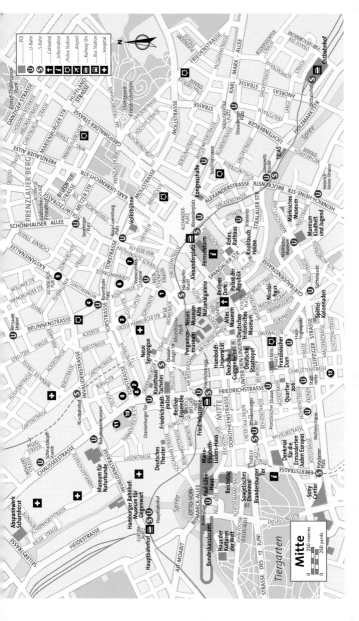

> ## BRANDENBURGER TOR (BRANDENBURG GATE)
> When the Berlin Wall came down in 1989, the everlasting symbol that stayed in the minds of all who watched the proceedings was the sight of the Brandenburg Gate hovering over the cheering masses of a newly unified Germany. After the dust settled, however, the West Germans quickly saw that the famed symbol of Prussian – and now German – power had been left to rot by the Eastern Bloc. Reunification brought a long-term restoration plan that left the gate gleaming. ❷ Pariser Platz Ⓝ U-Bahn/S-Bahn: Brandenburger Tor

❶ (030) 2026 9119 Ⓦ www.berlinerdom.de 🕐 09.00–20.00 Mon–Sat, 12.00–20.00 Sun, Apr–Sept; 09.00–19.00 Mon–Sat, 12.00–19.00 Sun, Oct–Mar Ⓝ S-Bahn: Hackescher Markt. Admission charge (extra for audio guide)

Das Denkmal für die Ermordeten Juden Europas
This commemorates the six million Jews who lost their lives in the Holocaust. The 'Memorial for the Murdered Jews of Europe' consists of an enormous sunken grid of 2,711 steles (commemorative concrete slabs or pillars), one for each page of the Talmud. Although it sounds simple, the end result is very powerful. ❷ Corner of Ebertstrasse & Behrenstrasse Ⓝ U-Bahn/S-Bahn: Brandenburger Tor

Neue Synagogue
No longer a working synagogue, the Neue Synagogue remains a symbol for the shattered past of Berlin's once-thriving Jewish

⬧ *The iconic, beautifully restored Brandenburg Gate*

community. It was built between 1857 and 1866, and was inaugurated in the presence of Bismarck. The beginning of the end arrived when the building was targeted by Nazis on Kristallnacht in 1938. An exhibition discussing Jewish life and the remains of the structure remind today's travellers of yesterday's tragedies. ⓐ Oranienburger Str. 28–30 ❶ (030) 8802 8300 ⓦ www.cjudaicum.de ⓛ 10.00–20.00 Sun & Mon, 10.00–18.00 Tues–Thur, 10.00–17.00 Fri, Apr–Sept; 10.00–20.00 Sun & Mon, 10.00–18.00 Tues–Thur, 10.00–14.00 Fri, Mar & Oct; 10.00–18.00 Sun & Mon, 10.00–18.00 Tues–Thur, 10.00–14.00 Fri, Nov–Feb ⓝ S-Bahn: Oranienburger Strasse. Admission charge

CULTURE

Alte Nationalgalerie

The speciality here is 19th-century art. A palatial building complete with sweeping staircases and a wonderful 'museumy' feel, the Alte Nationalgalerie consists of almost 500 pieces of important art from across Europe. While the focus is most definitely on German creativity, the collection also holds important Impressionist works from Manet, Monet and Rodin. Make sure you check out the masterpieces of German Romanticism on the top floor. ⓐ Bodestrasse 1–3 ❶ (030) 2090 5577 ⓦ www.smb.spk-berlin.de ⓛ 10.00–18.00 Tues, Wed & Fri–Sun, 10.00–22.00 Thur ⓝ U-Bahn/S-Bahn: Friedrichstrasse or Hackescher Markt. Admission charge

Altes Museum

Originally the only museum on the Museumsinsel, the Altes Museum is now primarily known for its temporary exhibitions. ⓐ Lustgarten ❶ (030) 2090 5577 ⓦ www.smb.spk-berlin.de ⓛ 10.00–18.00 Tues &

Wed, Fri–Sun, 10.00–22.00 Thur ⊘ S-Bahn: Hackescher Markt.
Admission charge

Deutsches Historisches Museum

The museum is focused around the core exhibition, which chronicles
specific important eras and dynasties in German history and their
relation to Europe and the world in general. ② Unter den Linden 2
① (030) 2030 4444 Ⓦ www.dhm.de ⊙ 10.00–18.00 ⊘ U-Bahn/
S-Bahn: Friedrichstrasse. Admission charge

Kunsthaus Tacheles

Originally a department store, after the Berlin Wall came down this
dilapidated building was used as a squat by artists. Inside you can
find art studios and exhibition spaces, a cinema, bar and ground floor

⬥ *The Altes Museum has great temporary exhibitions*

◆ *Some of the Pergamonmuseum treasures*

café (Café Zapata) – all collectively run. This is a prime example of Berlin's alternative culture. ⓐ Oranienburger Str. 53 ⓣ (030) 282 6185 ⓦ www.tacheles.de ⓛ Hours vary; call or simply pop in ⓝ U-Bahn: Oranienburger Tor

Neues Museum

Left in ruins by World War II, the beautiful Neues Museum re-opened in October 2009 and has wowed both crowds and critics with its blend of neoclassical heritage and modern architecture, the work of renowned architect David Chipperfield. Inside are exhibitions of prehistoric, classical and Egyptian antiquities. ⓐ Bodestrasse 3, Museumsinsel ⓣ (030) 2664 24242 ⓦ www.neues-museum.de ⓛ 10.00–18.00 Sun–Wed, 10.00–20.00 Thur–Sat ⓝ S-Bahn: Hackescher Markt. Admission charge

Pergamonmuseum

Named after the Hellenistic Pergamon Altar housed inside, the Pergamonmuseum is Berlin's answer to the British Museum and contains a vast collection of Greek and Islamic treasures plundered from its former colonies. ⓐ Am Kupfergraben ⓣ (030) 2090 5577 ⓦ www.smb.spk-berlin.de ⓛ 10.00–18.00 Fri–Wed, 10.00–22.00 Thur ⓝ S-Bahn: Hackescher Markt. Admission charge

RETAIL THERAPY

Mitte is Berlin's commercial centre. Head to Friedrichstrasse for designer threads and high fashion, and Hackescher Markt for trendy boutiques.

Bürgel-Haus This is distinctive blue-and-cream pottery from the state of Thüringen and will make an inexpensive, yet cosily German,

souvenir for friends back home. ⓐ Friedrichstrasse 154 ⓣ (030) 204 4519
ⓦ www.buergelhaus.de ⓛ 10.00–20.00 Mon–Sat, 12.00–18.00 Sun
ⓝ U-Bahn/S-Bahn: Friedrichstrasse

Claudia Skoda Modern fabrics and funky knitwear for the
adventurous lady or gentleman. ⓐ Alte Schönhauser Str. 35
ⓣ (030) 280 7211 ⓦ www.claudiaskoda.com ⓛ 11.30–19.30
Mon–Fri, 11.30–20.00 Sat ⓝ U-Bahn: Weinmeisterstrasse

Drykorn German fashion label Drykorn started out in 1996 with
specially tailored trousers; now it's expanded worldwide with a
range of classic and contemporary blazers, suits, dresses and coats.
ⓐ Neue Schönhauser Str. 14 (women's) & 6 (men's) ⓣ (030) 283 5010
ⓦ www.drykorn.com ⓛ 12.00–20.00 Mon–Fri, 12.00–19.00 Sat
ⓝ U-Bahn: Weinmeister Strasse

Erzgebirgskunst Original Johanna Gräf-Petzoldt wooden figurines,
musical boxes and lovely traditional German candle-mobiles.
ⓐ Sophienstrasse 9 ⓣ (030) 282 6754 ⓦ www.original-erzgebirgskunst.de
ⓛ 11.00–19.00 Mon–Fri, 11.00–20.00 Sat ⓝ U-Bahn: Weinmeisterstrasse

Galeries Lafayette The Berlin branch of the famed Parisian department
store. Stock is nothing to go gaga over, but the glass dome in the
lobby is truly inspiring. ⓐ Französische Str. 78 ⓣ (030) 209 480
ⓦ www.galerieslafayette.de ⓛ 10.00–20.00 Mon–Sat ⓝ U-Bahn:
Französische Str.

Neurotitan While it's a little tricky to find, this shop is worth it for
those interested in design, street art and visual communication.
Featuring hand-made books, zines and comics, as well as t-shirts,

postcards and prints by local designers, Neurotitan is a stalwart of the local creative scene. ⓐ Rosenthaler Str. 39 ⓣ (030) 3087 2576 ⓦ www.neurotitan.de ⓛ 12.00–20.00 Mon–Sat, 14.00–19.00 Sun ⓝ S-Bahn: Hackescher Markt

Quartier 206 A department store with a difference. Quartier 206 is the shop that upped Mitte in the style stakes with its selection of cutting-edge designer togs. Everything from Prada to Paul Smith, Dries Van Noten to Dolce is on offer. Staff are genuinely friendly. ⓐ Friedrichstrasse 71 ⓣ (030) 2094 6800 ⓦ www.quartier206.com ⓛ 11.00–20.00 Mon–Fri, 10.00–18.00 Sat ⓝ U-Bahn: Französische Str.

Stue Gorgeous modern Danish furniture and interior items, including restored vintage pieces. Antique Bang & Olufsen equipment is also in stock. ⓐ Torstrasse 70 ⓣ (030) 2472 7650 ⓛ 14.00–19.00 Mon–Sat ⓝ U-Bahn: Rosa-Luxemburg-Platz

TAKING A BREAK

Café Aedes £ ❶ Small and stylish, it's a great place to recharge in order to attack the rest of the shops in the Hackesche Hof neighbourhood. ⓐ Hof II, Hackesche Hof, Rosenthaler Str. 40–41 ⓣ (030) 285 8275 ⓦ www.cafe-aedes.de ⓛ 10.30–21.00 Mon–Thur; 10.30–23.00 Fri–Sun ⓝ S-Bahn: Hackescher Markt

Dada Falafel £ ❷ You won't be disappointed with the quality or the size of the servings. You can choose from a roll or plate of authentic Lebanese falafels, halloumi, fried aubergine or schawarma. ⓐ Linienstrasse 132 ⓣ (030) 2759 6927 ⓦ www.dadafalafel.de ⓛ 10.00–01.00 ⓝ U-Bahn: Oranienburger Tor

Fresh Eatery £ ❸ Asian-influenced rice-rolls, noodle dishes and soups – all made without artificial ingredients or flavourings. If you're thirsty try a fresh juice, tea, or Fair Trade coffee. ⓐ Auguststrasse 58 ❶ (030) 2219 8045 Ⓦ www.fresh-eatery.de ❶ 11.30–21.00 Ⓝ U-Bahn: Rosenthaler Platz

Gorki Park £ ❹ Russian-run café serving authentically Russian snacks, including *pierogi*, *blini* and *borscht*. ⓐ Weinbergsweg 25 ❶ (030) 448 7286 Ⓦ http://gorki-park.de ❶ 09.30–02.00 Ⓝ U-Bahn: Rosenthaler Platz

Der Imbiss £ ❺ The menu is delightfully fusion, featuring twists such as pizzas made with naan bread. A wonderful spot for fast food if you just can't face another *Currywurst*. ⓐ Kastanienallee 49 ❶ (030) 4302 0618 Ⓦ www.w-derimbiss.de ❶ 12.00–00.00 Ⓝ U-Bahn: Rosenthaler Platz

Chi Sing £–££ ❻ Fresh and flavoursome Vietnamese dishes in the heart of Mitte's hip shopping district. Great for vegetarians. ⓐ Rosenthaler Str. 62 ❶ (030) 2008 9284 Ⓦ www.chising-berlin.de ❶ 12.00–00.00 Ⓝ U-Bahn: Rosenthaler Platz

AFTER DARK

RESTAURANTS
Monsieur Vuong Indochina Cafe £ ❼ Although you may have trouble finding a table, staff are friendly, the restaurant is clean and stylish, and the food is fresh and tasty. ⓐ Alte Schönhauser Str. 46 ❶ (030) 9929 6924 Ⓦ www.monsieurvuong.de ❶ 12.00–00.00 Ⓝ U-Bahn: Weinmeisterstrasse

⬤ Hackescher Markt is great for a day's shopping or an evening out

Gambrinus £–££ ❽ No-nonsense German food. Think meat, cabbage and potato. Late opening times make it a perfect place for a bit of post-clubbing refuelling. ⓐ Linienstrasse 133 ❶ (030) 282 6043 ⓦ www.gambrinus-berlin-mitte.de ❸ 12.00–02.00 Sun–Thur, 12.00–04.00 Fri & Sat ⓝ U-Bahn: Oranienburger Tor

Tartane £–££ ❾ Although the cook moves at a slow pace, this tiny restaurant knows how to pack them in. The interior has a stylish GDR aesthetic and offers burgers that are worth the wait. No credit cards. ⓐ Torstrasse 225 ❶ (030) 4472 7036 ⓦ www.tartane.de ❸ 18.00–02.00 ⓝ U-Bahn: Oranienburger Tor

Good Time ££ ❿ If you've got a craving for spicy food, this restaurant serves up authentic Indonesian and Thai cuisine – not so easy to find in the land of stodge. ⓐ Chausseestrasse 1 ❶ (030) 2804 6015 ⓦ www.goodtime-berlin.de ❸ 12.00–00.00 ⓝ U-Bahn: Oranienburger Tor

Kellerrestaurant im Brecht-Haus ££ ⓫ For home-cooked dinner (well, playwright Bertolt Brecht's home at least), take a cultural trip to the Kellerrestaurant im Brecht-Haus. Everything available is derived from a list of Brecht's favourite dishes. Crammed full of stage memorabilia and treasures, dining here is a theatre buff's paradise. ⓐ Chausseestrasse 125 ❶ (030) 282 3843 ⓦ www.brechtkeller.de ❸ 18.00–00.00 ⓝ U-Bahn: Naturkundemuseum

Entrecote Fred's ££–£££ ⓬ Most diners come for just one thing – the incredible steak and frites. A well-stocked wine list is strictly French and covers most of the country. Service is quick and friendly. ⓐ Schutzenstrasse 5 ❶ (030) 2016 5496 ⓦ www.entrecote.de

🕐 12.00–00.00 Mon–Fri, 18.00–00.00 Sat, 18.00–23.00 Sun
Ⓝ U-Bahn: Stadtmitte

BARS & CLUBS

Bang Bang Club If you're in the mood for dancing, Bang Bang's DJs will sort you out with a mix of modern and 60s pop, rock and electro on almost any night of the week. You can also catch live touring bands from Germany, the USA, the UK and Australia. The staff are friendly, the music is loud and the 60s-inspired design is cool. Ⓐ Neue Promenade 10 Ⓣ (030) 6040 5310 Ⓦ www.bangbangclub.net 🕐 21.00–late Ⓝ S-Bahn: Hackescher Markt. Admission charge

B-flat This is one of Berlin's seminal jazz clubs featuring artists from all over the world. On any given night you might catch a jazz piano trio, a Latin-jazz fusion outfit or a big band. Ⓐ Rosenthaler Str. 13 Ⓣ (030) 283 3123 Ⓦ www.b-flat-berlin.de 🕐 21.00–late Ⓝ U-Bahn: Weinmeisterstrasse

Café Zapata Located in Berlin's most famous former squat, Tacheles, there's always something going on, from electronic laptop artists, to acoustic musos, DJs and live bands. Ⓐ Oranienburger Str. 54 Ⓣ (030) 281 6109 Ⓦ www.cafe-zapata.de 🕐 12.00–late; live music from 21.00 Ⓝ U-Bahn: Oranienburger Tor. Admission charge

Kaffee Burger Once the haunt of Prenzlauer Berg's literary underground, this GDR-focused club offers a mixed bag. Regular poetry and spoken word performances are interspersed with Russian disco nights to keep the gritty literary theme alive. Ⓐ Torstrasse 60 Ⓣ (030) 2804 6495 Ⓦ www.kaffeeburger.de 🕐 20.00–late Mon–Thur, 21.00–late Fri & Sat, 19.00–late Sun Ⓝ U-Bahn: Rosa-Luxemburg-Platz. Admission charge

Sage Club This club features three main spaces: a gothic/industrial/metal room, a live band (rock) room, and a chill-out area, complete with swimming pool. ⓐ Brückenstrasse 1 ⓣ (030) 2759 1080 ⓦ www.sage-club.de ⓛ 19.00–late Thur, 23.00–late Sun ⓝ U-Bahn: Heinrich-Heine-Strasse. Admission charge

Sophienclub A good night out if you want to dance but don't feel like dressing up. The resident DJs will treat you to party classics from disco, retro and alternative, to soul and R&B. ⓐ Sophienstrasse 6 ⓣ (030) 282 4552 ⓦ www.sophienclub-berlin.de ⓛ 23.00–late ⓝ U-Bahn: Weinmeisterstrasse; S-Bahn: Hackescher Markt. Admission charge

White Trash Fast Food This three-level extravaganza is a world of its own. From burlesque to country-trash, rockabilly, voodoo-blues and swing, the DJs and touring live acts are sure to entertain. ⓐ Schönhauser Allee 6-7 ⓣ (030) 5034 8668 ⓦ www.whitetrashfastfood.com ⓛ 12.00–late Mon–Fri, 18.00–late Sat & Sun ⓝ U-Bahn: Rosa-Luxemburg-Platz. Admission charge

THEATRES & CONCERT HALLS

Admiralspalast For over a century this majestic building has provided Berliners with entertainment – from a bowling alley and cinema to salt-water baths and a brothel. After falling into disrepair, it stood empty for ten years and has now been carefully restored. It offers a contemporary programme of cabaret, theatre, dance and music. ⓐ Friedrichstrasse 101 ⓣ (030) 4799 7499 ⓦ www.admiralspalast.de ⓛ From 19.00; check website for programme ⓝ U-Bahn/S-Bahn: Friedrichstrasse

Berliner Ensemble The house that Brecht built. The Berliner Ensemble is the jewel in Berlin's theatrical crown. This is the theatre that saw the premiere of Brecht's earliest works before his self-imposed exile in the USA. ⓐ Bertolt-Brecht-Platz 1 ⓣ (030) 2840 8155 ⓦ www.berliner-ensemble.de ⓛ Box office: 08.00–18.00 Mon–Fri, 11.00–18.00 Sat & Sun ⓝ U-Bahn/S-Bahn: Friedrichstrasse

Deutsches Theater Young directors, fresh talent and West End theatrical hits perform here, albeit strictly in German. ⓐ Schümannstrasse 13A ⓣ (030) 2844 1225 ⓦ www.deutschestheater.de ⓛ Box office: 11.00–18.30 Mon–Sat, 15.00–18.30 Sun ⓝ U-Bahn/S-Bahn: Friedrichstrasse

Komische Oper A small opera house with a focus on theatrical performance. Most performances are in German. ⓐ Behrenstrasse 55–57 ⓣ (030) 202 600 ⓦ www.komische-oper-berlin.de ⓛ Box office: 11.00–19.00 Mon–Sat, 13.00–16.00 Sun ⓝ U-Bahn/S-Bahn: Brandenburger Tor

Konzerthaus The best concert hall in town. Contemporary music is a speciality. ⓐ Gendarmenmarkt 2 ⓣ (030) 2030 921 01 ⓦ www.konzerthaus.de ⓛ Box office: 12.00–19.00 Mon–Sat, 12.00–16.00 Sun ⓝ U-Bahn: Französische Strasse

Staatsoper Unter den Linden The Staatsoper is the grande dame of opera halls in Berlin. Founded as the Royal Court Opera for Frederick the Great in 1742, the building is designed to resemble a Greek temple. ⓐ Unter den Linden 5–7 ⓣ (030) 2035 4555 ⓦ www.staatsoper-berlin.org ⓛ Box office: 12.00–19.00 ⓝ U-Bahn: Französische Str.

Prenzlauer Berg & Friedrichshain

Following the fall of the Wall, the twin districts of Prenzlauer Berg and Friedrichshain found themselves firmly in the spotlight. Capitalists fell in love with the financial prospect of purchasing dirt-cheap property and fixing it up for urban yuppies. Artists adored the idea of taking over a new neighbourhood to support their creative needs. Locals loved the idea of selling up for what they (at the time) thought was more money than they would ever see again. The result is Berlin's hottest region in which to work, play and live.

First to experience gentrification was Prenzlauer Berg. With its quaint, unrestored homes and leafy side streets, it was the shining jewel in the grimy East Berlin crown. Friedrichshain, due to its industrial look and feel, was originally a distant second but has now shot up in the 'most wanted' lists as property in Prenzlauer Berg becomes ever more scarce. Even international speculators are diving in, realising that the new Brandenburg Airport and efficient central train station are transforming the city into the European headquarters it has long striven to be.

Perhaps due to a decades-long lack of funding, neither neighbourhood is known for its sights. Rather, they are the districts tourists visit to experience the real Berlin – for it is here you'll find the city's best bars, clubs and most traditional restaurants.

Visitors often give this area a miss during the day, preferring to keep within the confines of the more museum-heavy regions of Mitte (see page 60) or Charlottenburg (see page 104). To do this would be to lose the opportunity of discovering the new Berlin – a city of mixed classes and cultures, Communist past and capitalist present.

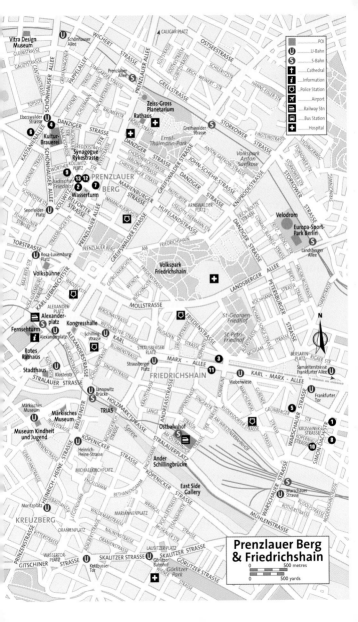

The night-time offers a plethora of opportunities. Many of the factories that drove the GDR machine were located in Friedrichshain and have since been converted into sizzling industrial-style nightclubs. Be sure to take taxis to and from these venues, as safety in the Eastern districts can be iffy after dark – especially in the maze-like industrial regions.

If you have had enough of culture and stuffy buildings, then Prenzlauer Berg is the best bet to while away a day. Locals are friendly and talkative – but be prepared to discuss your political views, as residents love a good debate over a beer (or ten). No matter what the end result is, you're sure to have made a new friend.

SIGHTS & ATTRACTIONS

Kollwitzplatz

The centre of the buzzing Prenzlauer Berg action, Kollwitzplatz is a pretty collection of pubs, cafés, restaurants and shops named after the 20th-century progressive graphic artist, Käthe Kollwitz. It was in this square that the first seeds of rebellion began when dissidents gathered in the Café Westphal during the early 1980s. ⓐ Kollwitzplatz Ⓝ U-Bahn: Senefelderplatz

Simon-Dach-Strasse

Take a stroll down Simon-Dach-Strasse and the surrounding streets in Friedrichshain. While this former East Berlin district is slowly being gentrified, it's still home to a strong anarchist-punk scene, and among the hip new bars and boutiques there are many beautiful crumbling old buildings. If you like people-watching, grab a table in one of the cafés and bars in which to sample the plentiful German beer, or enjoy a traditional Sunday brunch. Ⓝ U-Bahn/S-Bahn: Warschauer Strasse

⬥ See stars at the Zeiss-Gross Planetarium

Synagogue Rykestrasse

Once the only working synagogue in East Berlin, the Synagogue Rykestrasse was badly damaged during Kristallnacht in 1938. Left to rot by the Soviets until 1953, it is now the neighbourhood's place of worship. ⓐ Rykestrasse ⓦ www.synagoge-rykestrasse.de ⓛ Hours vary, depending on holidays and services ⓝ U-Bahn: Senefelderplatz

Volkspark Friedrichshain

The Volkspark provides a breath of fresh air in this largely industrial neighbourhood. Warm summer days transform this public space into a teeming mass of families. Socialist art and fairytale characters litter the lawns. ⓐ Friedenstrasse ⓝ U-Bahn: Schilling-Strasse

Zeiss-Gross Planetarium

The German capital's planetarium is smack bang in the heart of the city's trendiest neighbourhood. Seeing stars has never been easier as the complex is fitted out with state-of-the-art equipment. Unfortunately, the exhibits are in German only. Check the website for the monthly programme as the opening times vary. ⓐ Prenzlauer Allee 80 ⓣ (030) 4218 450 ⓦ www.sdtb.de ⓛ 09.00–12.00, 13.00–17.00 Tues–Thur, 13.00–17.00, 18.00–21.30 Fri, 14.30–21.00 Sat, 13.30–17.00 Sun ⓝ S-Bahn: Prenzlauer Allee. Admission charge

CULTURE

East Side Gallery

This open-air gallery is one of the few remaining stretches of the Berlin Wall still left standing – that wasn't boxed up and sold as Christmas stocking fillers in 1989. The artworks, which are dedicated to the promotion of peace, were restored in 2009 to celebrate

20 years since the fall of the Berlin Wall. ⓐ Mühlenstrasse
ⓦ www.eastsidegallery.com ⓝ U-Bahn/S-Bahn: Warschauer Strasse

KulturBrauerei

This former Schultheiss brewery is now a hub of activity and culture
in Prenzlauer Berg. Within its brick walls you'll find everything from
music stores to music venues, theatres, a beer garden, pool hall,
cafés and bars. Check the website for venues and opening hours.
ⓐ Schönhauser Allee 36 ⓣ (030) 443 5260 ⓦ www.kulturbrauerei-
berlin.de ⓝ U-Bahn: Eberswalder Strasse

RETAIL THERAPY

Everyone has their favourite pocket in Prenzlauer Berg and
Friedrichshain, and if you take a stroll around these neighbourhoods
you'll find boutiques filled with carefully crafted wares by local
designers. Take a walk down Kastanienallee and Oderberger Strasse
in Prenzlauer Berg, or Simon-Dach-Strasse in Friedrichshain and
you'll discover lots of gems tucked between cafés and bars. From
hand-made toys to jewellery and the latest in street fashion, Berlin's
creative scene has a lot to offer. If you have a craving for fresh fruit,
check out the organic food market held on Kollwitzplatz every
Thursday and Sunday. You could also pick up some picnic items
to eat in Volkspark Friedrichshain (see opposite).

Dick & Jane This boutique features stylish collections for men and
women, from Munich's Blank & Selig, to hats by Goorin, and hand-
made leather pieces from Wolfram Löhr. ⓐ Simon-Dach-Strasse 10
ⓣ (030) 2904 8994 ⓛ 12.00–20.00 Mon–Fri, 12.00–19.00 Sat
ⓝ U-Bahn: Frankfurter Tor

Eisdieler Fashion boutique owned and run by a collective of five up-and-coming designers. Styles include cutting-edge clubwear, comfortable casuals, second-hand finds and street duds. ❸ Kastanienallee 12 ❶ (030) 2839 1291 ❻ www.eisdieler.de ❺ 12.00–20.00 Mon–Fri, 12.00–19.00 Sat ❻ U-Bahn: Eberswalder Strasse

Furniture Retro furniture, TVs, radios, lamps and wallpaper from the 1960s and 70s. Burnt orange and brown are the major colours of choice. Austin Powers would love it. ❸ Sredzkistrasse 22 ❶ (030) 4434 2157 ❺ 12.30–19.00 Tues, 14.00–19.00 Wed, 12.30–20.00 Thur, 12.30–19.00 Fri, 12.30–16.00 Sat ❻ U-Bahn: Eberswalder Strasse

Mane Lange Korsetts It isn't every day you buy a corset – but if you've always wanted one, then this is the place to make a purchase. Choose from the selection off the rack or get one custom made. ❸ Hagenauer Str. 13 ❶ (030) 4432 8482 ❻ www.manelange.de ❺ Open by appointment only ❻ U-Bahn: Eberswalder Strasse

Misses & Marbles Enjoy a slice of home-baked cake while casting your eye across wares made by local Berlin designers in this cute combination of café and gift-shop. A great place to pick up a souvenir with a difference. ❸ Raumerstrasse 36 ❶ (030) 4978 6282 ❻ www.misses-marbles.de ❺ 10.00–19.00 Mon–Sat, 11.00–18.00 Sun ❻ U-Bahn: Eberswalder Strasse

Mondos Arts German souvenirs with a twist – this antique shop only stocks merchandise related to or directly from the East German, Cold War period. Propaganda posters, Soviet flags, army fatigues and pounding East German rock CDs make for unique

BERLIN'S BEST FLEA MARKET

This flea market is one of Berlin's biggest and most popular. Amongst the bric-a-brac and old clothes, you're sure to find a genuine German souvenir bargain of an ancient *bier stein* (tankard) or an artistic snapshot by a Berlin photographer. In the summer the locals sit in the sun drinking beer and chatting on the adjacent grassed area. You might catch live bands, drumming groups or jugglers practising their tricks.

Flohmarkt am Mauerpark 🏠 Bernauer Str. 63-64 (near the corner of Wolliner Strasse) 📞 (0179) 2925 0021 🌐 www.mauerparkmarkt.de 🕐 07.00–17.00 Sun 🚇 U-Bahn: Eberswalder Strasse

reminders of your visit. 🏠 Schreinerstrasse 6 📞 (030) 4201 0778 🌐 www.mondosarts.de 🕐 10.00–19.00 Mon–Fri, 12.00–17.00 Sat 🚇 U-Bahn: Samariterstrasse

MontK Equipment and clothing for serious outdoors types. Campers, skiers, climbers and canoeists will love it here. 🏠 Kastanienallee 83 📞 (030) 448 2590 🌐 www.mont-k.de 🕐 10.00–20.00 Mon–Fri, 10.00–18.00 Sat 🚇 U-Bahn: Eberswalder Strasse

Scuderi Original jewellery made on the premises by the three female owners. Gold, silver, pearls, stones and hand-blown glass are just some of the elements used to produce the innovative pieces. 🏠 Wörther Str. 32 📞 (030) 4737 4240 🌐 www.scuderi-schmuck.de 🕐 11.00–19.00 Mon–Fri, 11.00–16.00 Sat 🚇 U-Bahn: Senefelderplatz

Sexy Mama If you're pregnant it's easy to find comfortable clothes, but hard to find something that's a bit funky as well. Anne Cathrin-Petzold decided to solve this problem with her shop Sexy Mama.
ⓐ Lychener Str. 52 ① (030) 5471 4338 ⓦ www.sexy-mama.de
🕑 12.00–19.00 Mon, Thur & Fri, 10.00–19.00 Tues & Wed;
11.00–17.00 Sat ⓝ U-Bahn: Eberswalder Strasse

Sgt Peppers Fun vintage items from the 1960s to the 80s. The selection of airline bags is particularly whimsical. ⓐ Kastanianallee 91–92
① (030) 448 1121 ⓦ www.sgt-peppers-berlin.de 🕑 11.00–20.00
Mon–Sat ⓝ U-Bahn: Eberswalder Strasse

TAKING A BREAK

Café 100 Wasser £ ❶ Students and thrifty types love this place for its all-you-can-eat brunch buffet. Dishes are made fresh throughout the day to replenish what gets raided. ⓐ Simon-Dach-Strasse 39
① (030) 2900 1356 ⓦ www.cafe-100-wasser.de 🕑 09.00–01.00
Mon–Fri, 09.00–late Sat–Sun ⓝ U-Bahn: Frankfurter Tor

Café Anita Wronski £ ❷ Welcoming café on two levels. The place is spotlessly clean and quiet in the afternoon, making it a good place to sit down with a book and watch the world go by. ⓐ Knaackstrasse 26–28
① (030) 442 8483 🕑 09.00–02.00 ⓝ U-Bahn: Senefelderplatz

Café Ehrenburg £ ❸ Café and espresso bar named after the Russian/Jewish novelist, Ilja Ehrenburg. There are plenty of books available to skim while you sip a coffee or two. However, all will be from the pen of noted Commies, including Lenin, Stalin, Engels and Marx. ⓐ Karl-Marx-Allee 103 ① (030) 4210 5810 🕑 10.00–late ⓝ U-Bahn: Weberwiese

Konnopke's Imbiss £ ❹ The *Currywurst* is probably Berlin's greatest contribution to global cuisine and if you're in the mood for a sausage, this award-winning joint is one of the better – and oldest – places to try it. ❸ Schönhauser Allee 44A (under the U-Bahn tracks at the corner of Danziger Str. and Schönhauser Allee) ❶ (030) 442 7765 ⓦ http://konnopke-imbiss.de ⓛ 06.00–20.00 Mon–Fri, 12.00–19.00 Sat ⓝ U-Bahn: Eberswalder Strasse

Nil £ ❺ Sudanese *Imbiss* (fast food) joint serving up lamb and chicken dishes for those on the go (no tables). Dig into the halloumi, falafel or aubergine salad. ❸ Grünberger Str. 52 ❶ (030) 2904 7713 ⓦ www.nil-imbiss.de ⓛ 10.00–00.00 ⓝ U-Bahn: Frankfurter Tor

Prater Biergarten £ ❻ Opened in 1837, this is Berlin's oldest beer garden. Located in a courtyard of leafy chestnut trees, it's a good place to stop for a break after a morning of roaming Berlin's streets. ❸ Kastanienallee 7-9 ❶ (030) 448 5688 ⓦ www.pratergarten.de ⓛ 12.00–late Apr–Sept ⓝ U-Bahn: Eberswalder Strasse

AFTER DARK

RESTAURANTS
Suriya Kanthi £ ❼ Specialising in Sri Lankan and South Indian cuisine, this restaurant offers vegetarians a welcome respite in the land of *Wurst*. Try the delicious curries or the coconut milk pancakes. Cash only. ❸ Knaackstrasse 4 ❶ (030) 442 5301 ⓦ www.suriya-kanthi.de ⓛ 12.00–01.00 Mon–Sat, 11.00–16.00 Sun ⓝ Tram: M2 to Knaackstrasse

Alarabi £–££ ❽ In the heart of hip Friedrichshain, Alarabi offers a great Middle-Eastern menu featuring dishes from Iraq, Lebanon and

Syria. Alternatively, just pull up a couch and settle in for a session with a hookah pipe. Ten flavoured tobaccos are available. **ⓐ** Krossener Str. 19 **ⓣ** (030) 2977 1995 **ⓛ** 12.00–00.00 Mon–Thu, 10.00–01.00 Fri–Sun **ⓜ** U-Bahn: Frankfurter Tor; tram: M8 to Libauer Strasse

Mao Thai £–££ ❾ Colourful interiors and fresh ingredients make this one of the most popular Thai restaurants in town. The menu is extensive and the dishes are authentic. **ⓐ** Wörther Str. 30 **ⓣ** (030) 441 9261 **ⓛ** 12.00–23.30 **ⓜ** U-Bahn: Senefelderplatz

Miseria e Nobiltà £–££ ❿ This authentic Italian restaurant is always packed. Family-owned and run, you'll be treated to Grandma's special recipes. Vegetarian options available. **ⓐ** Kopernikusstrasse 16 **ⓣ** (030) 2904 9249 **ⓛ** 17.30–00.00 Tues–Thur, Sun, 17.30–01.00 Fri & Sat **ⓜ** U-Bahn/S-Bahn: Warschauer Strasse

Prager Hopfenstube £–££ ⓫ Czech cuisine is probably one of the few that can give German dishes a run for their money on the stodge front. Typical choices include dumplings, roast pork and fresh sauerkraut. Even the vegetarians can't get away from the fat fest – one of the tastiest treats is deep-fried cheese served with remoulade sauce and chips. What makes this place special is its location on what was once the main drag of East Berlin. **ⓐ** Karl-Marx-Allee 127 **ⓣ** (030) 426 7367 **ⓛ** 11.00–00.00 **ⓜ** U-Bahn: Weberwiese

Pasternak ££ ⓬ Crammed with people tucking into authentic *borscht* and *stroganoff*, this Russian eatery has pretty typical Russian service and music as well. **ⓐ** Knaackstrasse 22–24 **ⓣ** (030) 441 3399 **ⓦ** www.restaurant-pasternak.de **ⓛ** 10.00–01.00 **ⓜ** U-Bahn: Senefelderplatz

Zander ££–£££ ❸ A family-run restaurant offering fine German cooking with an emphasis on game and fish dishes. Come on Sundays to see how Germans do a Sunday roast. ⓐ Kollwitzstrasse 50 ⓣ (030) 4405 7678 ⓦ www.zander-restaurant.de ⓛ 18.00–late Tues–Sun ⓝ U-Bahn: Senefelderplatz

BARS & CLUBS

Berghain/Panorama Bar Touted by many as the best techno club around, this industrial-sized club is located in a massive concrete structure (formerly a power station). Berlin's straight and gay crowds converge here for the purpose of hardcore partying. Not for the faint-hearted. Strict door policy. ⓐ Am Wriezenerbahnhof ⓦ www.berghain.de ⓛ 00.00–late Fri & Sat ⓝ S-Bahn: Ostbahnhof. Admission charge

⬥ *An original stretch of the Berlin Wall at the East Side Gallery*

Fritz Club im Postbahnhof Dance the night away to indie-rock or pop tunes, or check out a live band. ⓐ Strasse der Pariser Kommune 8 ⓣ (030) 698 1280 ⓦ www.fritzclub.com ⓛ Live bands from 20.00; club nights from 23.00 ⓝ U-Bahn: Ostbahnhof. Admission charge

Icon Good breakbeat and drum 'n' bass bar with a bumping dancefloor. ⓐ Cantianstrasse 15 ⓣ (030) 3229 70520 ⓦ www.iconberlin.de ⓛ 23.00–late Tues, 23.30–late Fri & Sat ⓝ U-Bahn: Eberswalder Strasse. Admission charge

K17 This warehouse complex features a labyrinth of live venues for touring goth and metal bands, and dark bars with DJs spinning industrial, new wave and 80s tracks. ⓐ Pettenkoferstrasse 17A ⓣ (030) 4208 9300 ⓦ www.k17.de ⓛ DJs: 22.00–late Fri & Sat; bands: usually 18.00 or 19.00; check the website for programme ⓝ U-Bahn/S-Bahn: Frankfurter Allee. Admission charge

Maria am Ostbahnhof This warehouse is located next to the river Spree and is one of Berlin's main clubs for house, techno and all things electronic. Check the website for live acts and DJs. ⓐ An der Schillingbrücke ⓣ (030) 2123 8190 ⓦ www.clubmaria.de ⓛ 23.00–late Fri & Sat; check programme for occasional Thursday opening ⓝ S-Bahn: Ostbahnhof. Admission charge

Nbi With its retro lounge-style interior and diverse programme, Nbi is a popular student hangout. You might find yourself stepping up for a game of table tennis or Kicker, listening to a quirky indie band from Europe or the US, or getting down to disco tunes from the energetic DJs. ⓐ Schönhauser Allee 36 ⓦ www.neueberlinerinitiative.de ⓛ 20.00–late ⓝ U-Bahn: Eberswalder Strasse. Admission charge

YAAM Standing for Young and African Arts Market, this is Berlin's premier venue for German and international dub, reggae and dancehall DJs and live acts. You'll find YAAM just at the end of the East Side Gallery, right next to the river Spree. ⓐ Stralauer Platz 35 ⓣ (030) 615 1354 ⓦ www.yaam.de ⓛ 13.00–late May–Sept; 23.00–late Oct–Apr; live music usually from 23.00 but check website for details ⓝ S-Bahn: Ostbahnhof. Admission charge

CINEMAS & THEATRES

Brotfabrik During the GDR period, this former bread factory was used as a youth centre. Today, the structure holds a café, cinema and experimental theatre that hosts fringe-focused work in a variety of languages. ⓐ Caligariplatz ⓣ (030) 471 4001 ⓦ www.brotfabrik-berlin.de ⓛ Hours vary; check website for programme ⓝ Tram: M2, M12 or M13 to Prenzlauer Allee or Ostseestrasse

Prater Intriguing theatre under the direction of the much larger Volksbühne. Artistic Director Rene Pollesch is carving out a name for the venue. Expect to be challenged. ⓐ Kastanienallee 79 ⓣ (030) 240 655 ⓦ www.volksbuehne-berlin.de ⓛ Box office: 12.00–18.00 ⓝ U-Bahn: Eberswalder Strasse ⓘ Undergoing renovations until mid-2011; call for update

Theater unterm Dach New German fringe work performed in the attic of a converted factory. The artistic director scours the country looking for promising directors, companies and playwrights, so the results can be very positive. ⓐ Danziger Str. 101 ⓣ (030) 9029 53817 ⓦ www.theateruntermdach-berlin.de ⓛ Box office: 19.00–20.00 on show evenings ⓝ Tram: M4 to Greifswalder Strasse or Danziger Strasse

Kreuzberg & Schöneberg

In the days when the city was split in two, Kreuzberg and
Schöneberg were at the cutting edge of cool. The more affordable
districts of Prenzlauer Berg and Friedrichshain may since have
stolen that mantle from the region, but a true sense of community
remains amongst its residents. Both neighbourhoods house large
minority populations. Schöneberg has traditionally acted as the
unofficial headquarters of the gay community, while Kreuzberg
houses the Turkish population and a scattering of artists left over
from the days when the region was a massive squatter's paradise.

Noted artists have been drawn to both regions time and time
again, attracted by the warmth and creativity of residents. David
Bowie, Iggy Pop and Christopher Isherwood are just a few of the
bigger names. In fact, it was while living in Kreuzberg that Isherwood
concocted the legendary character of Sally Bowles in his series of
stories set in Berlin. Marlene Dietrich was also a regular visitor
during her early years, frequently spotted living it large in the
artistic salons and bars surrounding Nollendorfplatz. The only
Marlenes you'll find these days will be female impersonators,
as the streets surrounding this square now house the local
gay village.

While prices have risen and the two areas are decidedly
upmarket, shopping in both neighbourhoods remains a treat. Unlike
Charlottenburg (see page 104) and Mitte (see page 60), the districts
have shunned chain shops in favour of unique boutiques. What you
will find is a diverse range of places to part with hard-earned cash,
with everything from antique radios to authentic art deco furniture
available at competitive prices. Be warned that opening hours can
be bizarre owing to the nature of the area's shop owners.

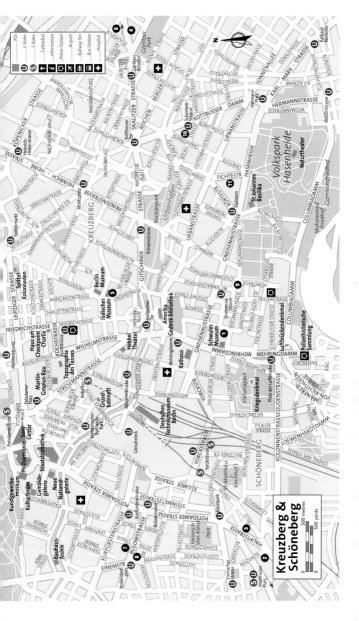

SIGHTS & ATTRACTIONS

Gruselkabinett

Part historically fascinating Nazi-era bunker, part Halloween-themed scary monster fun world, Gruselkabinett is popular both with historically minded tourists and excitable teenagers looking for a shock. Downstairs is where the displays dedicated to medieval torture techniques and Nazi artefacts are kept, while upstairs is a big, scary maze with ghosts and creatures of the night. ⓐ Schöneberger Str. 23A ❶ (030) 2655 5546 ⓦ www.gruselkabinett-berlin.de ❺ 10.00–15.00 Mon, 10.00–19.00 Tues, Thur, Sun, 10.00–20.00 Fri, 12.00–20.00 Sat Ⓝ S-Bahn: Anhalter Bahnhof. Admission charge

⬤ Checkpoint Charlie was the crossing point between East and West Berlin

Topographie des Terrors

Site of the former Gestapo headquarters, the Topographie des Terrors stands where the Holocaust was dreamt up and executed by the Nazi regime. Small markers dot the area showing visitors the location of important landmarks in the original complex. A stunning new exhibition centre opened on the site in 2010, with fascinating displays that chronicle the state-sponsored terror.
ⓐ Niederkirchnerstrasse 8 ⓣ (030) 2545 0950 ⓦ www.topographie.de ⓛ 10.00–20.00 May–Sept, 10.00–dusk Oct–Apr ⓜ U-Bahn/S-Bahn: Potsdamer Platz

HAUS AM CHECKPOINT CHARLIE

In existence almost from the time the first piece of barbed wire was put in place to separate the city, the Haus am Checkpoint Charlie has been acting as Berlin's social and political conscience from its inception. Before the fall of the Wall, the museum was dedicated to providing information about the atrocities happening behind the Iron Curtain and staff worked towards the Wall's demise. After the fall, the Haus am Checkpoint Charlie went through a bit of an adjustment period. It has now emerged as a wonderful collection of historically significant Wall memorabilia, including information about the ways in which determined protestors and regular folk helped tear it down. The Wall may no longer stand, but the Haus am Checkpoint Charlie's importance and interest remains.
ⓐ Friedrichstrasse 43–45 ⓣ (030) 253 7250 ⓦ www.mauer-museum.de ⓛ 09.00–22.00 ⓜ U-Bahn: Kochstrasse. Admission charge

CULTURE

Deutsches Technikmuseum Berlin

Dedicated to telling the story of German industry, this museum is housed in the former goods depot of the Anhalter Bahnhof. Rail exhibits are the showcase items, but you'll also find displays dedicated to street advancements, water, air traffic, computers, printing technology and jewellery. There's really something here for everyone, including lots of hands-on exhibits that are entertaining for both adults and kids. ⓐ Trebbiner Str. 9 ⓣ (030) 902 540 ⓦ www.sdtb.de ⓛ 09.00–17.30 Tues–Fri, 10.00–18.00 Sat & Sun ⓝ U-Bahn: Möckernbrücke. Admission charge

Jüdisches Museum

If you have time for just one museum while you are in town, then make it this one. When Daniel Libeskind's Jewish Museum was completed in 1998, it was the final step in a journey that began back in 1971, when the city's Jewish community celebrated its 300th anniversary. The Jewish Museum outlines the growth of Judaism in Germany and its importance from the early days of the Middle Ages straight through to modern day. One of the most heartbreaking displays is that of the Weimar Republic. Jews had achieved absolute equality during this seemingly bright period in German Jewish history. The images of cheerful Jewish families and politicians enjoying unheard-of freedoms during this golden age stay in the mind, especially when compared with horrific pictures of freed concentration camp victims. ⓐ Lindenstrasse 9–14 ⓣ (030) 2599 3300 ⓦ www.jmberlin.de ⓛ 10.00–22.00 Mon, 10.00–20.00 Tues–Sun ⓝ U-Bahn: Hallesches Tor. Admission charge

◐ *Steel yourself for a visit to the Jüdisches Museum*

Martin-Gropius-Bau

Constantly changing art exhibits are displayed in this massive wedding-cake of a structure named after its original architect. Although it was originally built back in 1881, the exhibitions it hosts are generally cutting-edge and definitely worth a look. ⓐ Niederkirchnerstrasse 7 ⓣ (030) 254 860 ⓦ www.gropiusbau.de ⓛ 10.00–20.00 May–early Aug; 10.00–20.00 Wed–Mon, early Aug– Apr ⓝ S-Bahn: Anhalter Bahnhof. Admission charge

Schwules Museum

The only museum in the world dedicated to homosexuality. The ever-changing exhibitions chronicle gay culture and have proven to be a hit with the local populace. Be warned: some of the art on display can be decidedly risqué and a challenge to explain to children. ⓐ Mehringdamm 61 ⓣ (030) 6959 9050 ⓦ www.schwulesmuseum.de ⓛ 14.00–18.00 Mon, Wed–Fri, Sun, 14.00–19.00 Sat ⓝ U-Bahn: Mehringdamm. Admission charge

RETAIL THERAPY

As both Kreuzberg and Schöneberg are heavily residential, many of the boutiques found here are one-offs and very community-oriented. Few chains and high street names can be found within either district's confines. Markets are designed to cater to the needs of locals, specifically the Farmers' Market held weekdays on Wittenbergplatz and the multicultural Winterfeldt Markt held every Saturday. Both markets offer great opportunities to pick up *Wurst*, enjoy a coffee or catch up on gossip.

Belladonna Natural cosmetics for women with a conscience. Product lines represented include Weleda, Lavera, Logona and Dr Hauschka.

ⓐ Bergmannstrasse 101 ⓣ (030) 694 3731 ⓦ www.bella-donna.de
ⓛ 10.00–19.00 Mon–Fri, 10.00–18.00 Sat ⓝ U-Bahn: Mehringdamm

Colours Vintage finds can be picked up for a song at this great
second-hand boutique. The bulk of the merchandise is your basic
jeans-and-t-shirts combos. Other finds can include *Dirndls* (German
peasant-style dresses) and the occasional cocktail gown from the
50s and 60s. ⓐ 1st courtyard, Bergmannstrasse 102 ⓣ (030) 694 3348
ⓦ www.kleidermarkt.de ⓛ 11.00–19.00 Mon–Fri, 12.00–19.00 Sat
ⓝ U-Bahn: Mehringdamm

Mobilien This is a colourfully kitsch (yet contemporary) home
furnishings store created by two Berlin designers. Check out their
range of hand-painted toasters, monster-themed plates and wall
tattoos. ⓐ Goltzstrasse 13b ⓣ (030) 2362 4940 ⓦ www.mobilien-
berlin.de ⓛ 11.00–19.00 Mon–Fri, 10.00–17.00 Sat ⓝ U-Bahn:
Eisenacher Strasse

Molotow Designer clothes and accessories for men and women
by local designers. You'll certainly blow your friends away with a
dress or suit from here. ⓐ Gneisenaustrasse 112 ⓣ (030) 693 0818
ⓦ www.molotowberlin.de ⓛ 13.00–18.00 Mon–Fri, 12.00–16.00 Sat
ⓝ U-Bahn: Mehringdamm

Radio Art Antique radios are the only things on offer at this
quirky shop. It may sound boring, but they're actually a lot more
fascinating than you might think. Note the strange opening hours
to avoid disappointment. ⓐ Zossener Str. 2 ⓣ (030) 693 9435
ⓦ www.radio-art.de ⓛ 12.00–18.00 Thur & Fri, 10.00–13.00 Sat
ⓝ U-Bahn: Gneisenaustrasse

TURKISH MARKET

Take a stroll down to the Turkish market in Kreuzberg which takes place every Tuesday and Friday. You'll find stalls selling everything from fresh cheese, bread, fruit and vegetables, to fabric, ribbons and socks. It starts at the corner of Kottbusserdamm and Maybachufer, and continues down alongside the Landwehr canal. 🕐 11.00–18.30 Tues & Fri 🚇 U-Bahn: Kottbusser Tor

Soultrade – Scratch Records If you have a vinyl addiction and a penchant for black music, you have to check out this record store. They've got funk, soul, hip hop, R&B, jazz, Brazilian music and much more. 🏠 Zossener Str. 31 📞 (030) 694 5257 🌐 www.soultrade.de 🕐 11.00–20.00 Mon–Sat 🚇 U-Bahn: Gneisenaustrasse

Tiki Heart Clothes and accessories for those into rock, punk and rockabilly. Among the classic creepers, you'll also find merchandise for bands like Motörhead and the Buzzcocks. Check out the Tiki Heart Café upstairs or go and see some live music at Wild at Heart next door. 🏠 Wiener Str. 20 📞 (030) 6107 4703 🌐 www.tikiheart.de 🕐 11.00–20.00 Mon–Sat 🚇 U-Bahn: Görlitzer Bahnhof

TAKING A BREAK

Atlantic £ ❶ By day this café buzzes with breakfast and lunch specials. By night it becomes a beer den. Outdoor tables go fast during the summer months. 🏠 Bergmannstrasse 100 📞 (030) 691 9292 🕐 09.00–01.00 🚇 U-Bahn: Gneisenaustrasse

Bilderbuch £ ❷ Book-lined café that is absolutely vast. Don't be put off by the entrance, which makes it look like a second-hand bookseller; go further inside to uncover the spacious tables. The location makes it a great rest stop if you happen to be shopping in Schöneberg. ⓐ Akazienstrasse 28 ❶ (030) 7870 6057 ⓦ www.cafe-bilderbuch.de ❶ 09.00–01.00 Mon–Fri, 10.00–01.00 Sat & Sun ⓝ U-Bahn: Eisenacher Strasse

Jot £ ❸ Combining a sleek and airy interior with a relaxed vibe, this sandwich shop is popular with locals. Try the focaccia with Italian meatballs. ⓐ Crellestrasse 41 ❶ (030) 7800 1562 ⓦ www.jotonline.eu ❶ 09.00–18.00 Mon–Sat, 12.00–18.00 Sun ⓝ U-Bahn: Kleistpark

Salon Schmück £ ❹ This combination café/second-hand clothing shop allows you to browse while you brunch. The muffins and bagels are deliciously fresh, as are the juices. Those looking for something a little stronger can choose from the excellent beer, wine and cocktail list. ⓐ Skalitzer Str. 80 ❶ (030) 6900 4775 ❶ 09.00–02.00 Mon–Fri, 10.00–02.00 Sat & Sun ⓝ U-Bahn: Schlesisches Tor

Liebermanns £–££ ❺ The (non-kosher) restaurant of the Jewish Museum serves up traditional entrées and pastries buffet-style. ⓐ Lindenstrasse 9–14 ❶ (030) 2593 9760 ⓦ www.licbermanns.de ❶ 10.00–22.00 Mon, 10.00–20.00 Tues–Sun ⓝ U-Bahn: Hallesches Tor

AFTER DARK

RESTAURANTS

Sao Mai £ ❻ This cute restaurant serves up Vietnamese classics like Pho Bo soup and fresh rolls, but if you're feeling a little adventurous,

go for the yellow catfish. Ⓐ Nollendorfstrasse 8 ☎ (030) 216 6698
🌐 www.saomai-berlin.de 🕐 11.30–22.30 Ⓝ U-Bahn: Nollendorfplatz

Bejte Ethiopia £–££ ❼ This Ethiopian establishment is very
homey. A good place for a messy, yet filling, night out. Dishes include
a variety of stewed, spiced meats and vegetables. Ⓐ Zietenstrasse 8
☎ (030) 262 5933 🌐 www.bejte-ethiopia.de 🕐 16.00–01.00 Mon–Fri,
14.00–02.00 Sat & Sun (kitchen closes 21.00) Ⓝ U-Bahn: Nollendorfplatz

Cuno £–££ ❽ This restaurant serves up a menu of Japanese and
Vietnamese food ranging from sushi to noodles and rice dishes with
fusion twists. If you're feeling adventurous why not try the Italian sushi.
Vegetarians are catered for. Ⓐ Schlesische Str. 5 ☎ (030) 6951 8463
🌐 www.berlin-cuno.de 🕐 12.00–00.00 Ⓝ U-Bahn: Schlesisches Tor

Austria ££ ❾ For a taste of old oom-pah-pah, drag your *Lederhosen*
down to Austria. Resembling a German hunting lodge inside, complete
with deer antlers and wooden-beamed ceilings, Austria dishes up hearty
German food with a strong focus on meat. Everything is organic.
The schnitzel is overwhelmingly excellent. Ⓐ Bergmannstrasse 30
☎ (030) 694 4440 🕐 18.00–late Ⓝ U-Bahn: Gneisenaustrasse

Café Avril ££ ❿ In a city where sausage is king, Café Avril makes a nice
change. You won't see a speck of *speck* (bacon) at this vegetarian
Mediterranean-influenced restaurant (although they do serve fish).
And this is one place you can take the kids as there's a special menu
section and even a play room. Ⓐ Graefestrasse 83 ☎ (030) 6273 5398
🌐 www.cafe-avril.com 🕐 09.00–02.00 Mon–Fri, 10.00–02.00 Sat
& Sun Ⓝ U-Bahn: Schönleinstrasse

Le Cochon Bourgeois ££ ⓫ Quality French food rounded off with a wine menu strong on bottles from the Alsace region. Dishes can be heavy and are therefore better for winter evenings. ⓐ Fichtestrasse 24 ⓣ (030) 693 0101 ⓦ www.lecochon.de ⓛ 18.00–01.00 Tues–Sat ⓝ U-Bahn: Südstern

BARS & CLUBS

Goya The extravagant façade and grandiose interior make Goya an impressive location to party. DJs mix house and techno classics with R&B. ⓐ Nollendorfplatz 5 ⓣ (030) 4199 39000 ⓦ www.goya-berlin.com ⓛ 23.00–late Sat; occasionally open Fri – check website ⓝ U-Bahn: Nollendorfplatz. Admission charge

⬤ *Check out one of Kreuzberg's many cool bars*

Lido This venue houses one of the best purpose-built sound-systems in the city, which does justice to the range of live acts and DJs who play here. Check the website for acts ranging from pop to soul, hip hop, rock or breakbeat. Cuvrystrasse 7 (030) 7895 8410 www.lido-berlin.de Usually 21.00–late Thur–Sat U-Bahn: Schlesisches Tor. Admission charge

SO36 Depending on the night, you might catch a ska, hardcore or punk band, a flea market, bingo or karaoke night, or even a Middle-Eastern gay dance party. Best to check the website for details. Oranienstrasse 190 (030) 6140 1306 www.so36.de 20.00–late U-Bahn: Görlitzer Bahnhof. Admission charge

Watergate Spacious, glass-fronted club good for a cocktail (or five). The views of the Spree are enjoyable (especially in summer) while you dance to the minimal house, techno and assorted electronic soundtrack. If you want to relax, be sure to go to the basement lounge. Falckensteinstrasse 49 (030) 6128 0396 www.water-gate.de 00.00–late Wed, Fri & Sat U-Bahn: Schlesisches Tor. Admission charge

CINEMAS & THEATRES
Eiszeit The theatre of choice for film freaks. Programming includes Japanimation, American indie flicks, Hong Kong martial arts movies and everything in between – all in their original languages. Zeughofstrasse 20 (030) 611 6016 www.eiszeit-kino.de U-Bahn: Görlitzer Bahnhof

English Theatre Berlin The city's only English-language theatre specialises in fringe productions. Fidicinstrasse 40 Box office:

(030) 691 1211 Ⓦ www.etberlin.de Ⓛ Varies, so phone to check
Ⓝ U-Bahn: Platz der Luftbrücke

HAU 1-2-3 Make sure you check the programme at all three HAU theatres – Eins (1), Zwei (2) and Drei (3) – as all of them have exciting productions to offer at different times of the year. Tickets can be purchased from the central box office at HAU 2 or on the door up to one hour before the event. It presents challenging, provocative performance and dance. Ⓐ HAU 1: Stresemannstrasse 29; HAU 2: Hallesches Ufer 32; HAU 3: Tempelhofer Ufer 10 Ⓣ (030) 2590 0427 Ⓦ www.hebbel-am-ufer.de Ⓛ Box office: 12.00–19.00 Ⓝ U-Bahn: Hallesches Tor

Kleine Nachtrevue The closest thing these days to the original Berlin cabaret. Shows are saucy, tongue in cheek, risqué and filled with a special brand of Berliner humour. The weekend shows starting at 21.00 are a mixed bag of drag and erotic acts – go mid-week for the fun and frivolity. After the show starts at 21.00 there's no admittance. Ⓐ Kurfürstenstrasse 116 Ⓣ (030) 218 8950 Ⓦ www.kleine-nachtrevue.de Ⓛ 20.00–late Wed–Sat Ⓝ U-Bahn: Wittenbergplatz

Odeon One of the few English-language-specific cinemas in town. As it is a traditional single-screen cinema, the surroundings are plush. No cramped seats or obscured views here. Ⓐ Hauptstrasse 116 Ⓣ (030) 7870 4019 Ⓦ www.yorck.de Ⓛ Hours vary: check website Ⓝ U-Bahn/S-Bahn: Innsbrucker Platz

Charlottenburg & Tiergarten

Formerly the heart of West Berlin, Charlottenburg and Tiergarten were the districts of choice for the post-war, pre-reunification bourgeoisie. While most of the hipness and history have moved to points east, their popularity remains – especially among conservative professionals and families.

Greener and leafier than their eastern counterparts, both districts are packed with cultural landmarks, including the seat of German government, the Reichstag (see below). The Tiergarten (see page 107), one of Europe's largest urban parks, is worshipped by locals, while a walk along Kurfürstendamm remains the height of chic. The further west you go on this expensive stretch of real estate, the more exclusive it gets.

SIGHTS & ATTRACTIONS

Kaiser Wilhelm Gedächtniskirche

Once one of Berlin's most active places of worship, the Kaiser Wilhelm Gedächtniskirche was destroyed by Allied bombs during the height of World War II. The church still stands – just about – as a reminder of the effects of war. Adjoining it is a new church that's constructed of concrete and blue glass mosaic, which bathes the neighbourhood in a soothing glow after dark. ❸ Breitscheidplatz ❶ (030) 218 5023 ❼ www.gedaechtniskirche-berlin.de ❺ 09.00–19.00 ❹ U-Bahn/ S-Bahn: Zoologischer Garten

Reichstag

No structure holds more historical significance in Berlin than the Reichstag. It was on this spot on 17 February 1933 that the Nazis took

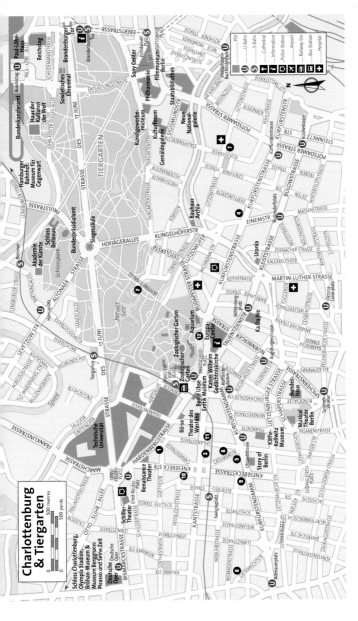

control of the German government by burning down the Reichstag building, then blaming it on the Communist Party. The Reichstag is once more the seat of government. The inspiring glass dome designed by Sir Norman Foster provides wonderful views over Tiergarten, but if you are thinking of taking a look up the top, go early – the queues can be very long. ⓐ Platz der Republik 1, off Scheidemannstrasse ⓣ (030) 2273 2152 ⓦ www.bundestag.de ⓛ 08.00–00.00 (last entry 22.00) Ⓝ U-Bahn/S-Bahn: Brandenburger Tor

Schloss Charlottenburg

Impressive in size and grandeur, this palace was built in the late 17th and early 18th centuries by Frederick III, Elector of Brandenburg, in a mix of baroque and rococo styles. Those interested in history will want to tour the state apartments and reception rooms, while others can content themselves with a stroll around the formal gardens and expansive grounds. ⓐ Luisenplatz & Spandauer Damm ⓣ (030) 320 911 ⓦ www.spsg.de ⓛ Palace: 10.00–18.00 Tues–Sun, Apr–Oct; 10.00–17.00 Tues–Sun, Nov–Mar; wing: 10.00–18.00 Wed–Mon, Apr–Oct; 10.00–17.00 Wed–Mon, Nov–Mar Ⓝ Bus: M45 to Schloss Charlottenburg. Admission charge (grounds free)

Siegessäule

Built in 1873, this column commemorates the Prussian military success over Denmark, Austria and France. A gilded Goddess of Victoria stands at the top surrounded by captured French cannons and cannonballs. Visitors can climb the 285 steps to enjoy the views over the city. ⓐ Str. des 17 Juni ⓣ (030) 391 2961 ⓦ www.monument-tales.de ⓛ 09.30–18.30 Mon–Fri, 09.30–19.00 Sat & Sun, Apr–Oct; 10.00–17.00 Mon–Fri, 10.00–17.30 Sat & Sun, Nov–Mar Ⓝ S-Bahn: Bellevue. Admission charge

OLYMPIA STADION

The stadium of the 1936 Olympics was made famous by two things: the triumphs of sprinter Jesse Owens, who won four gold medals, and *Olympia*, a documentary of the Games made by Leni Riefenstahl, infamous for her compelling record of a rally at Nuremberg, *Triumph des Willens* (*Triumph of the Will*). Built in the epic style loved by all Nazis, the stadium was restored in time to host matches for the 2006 World Cup. ⓐ Olympischer Platz 3 ⓣ (030) 3068 8100 ⓦ www.olympiastadion-berlin.de ⓛ 09.00–19.00, mid-Mar–May; 09.00–20.00 June–mid-Sept; 09.00–19.00 mid-Sept–Oct; 09.00–16.00 Nov–mid-Mar ⓝ U-Bahn: Olympia Stadion. Admission charge

Story of Berlin

The city's history told through interactive displays, talking headsets and wax mannequins. It's a lot more interesting than it sounds. You even get to tour an original nuclear bomb shelter hidden under Kurfürstendamm. ⓐ Kurfürstendamm 207–208 ⓣ (030) 8872 0157 ⓦ www.story-of-berlin.de ⓛ 10.00–20.00 (last entry 18.00) ⓝ U-Bahn: Uhlandstrasse. Admission charge

Tiergarten

Berlin's rural heart is the Tiergarten. This sprawling mass of wooded parkland is loved by Berliners, as it offers up hiking trails, bike paths and rowboats to one and all. On warm days, office workers make a beeline for the grass to enjoy picnic lunches. ⓝ S-Bahn: Tiergarten

Zoologischer Garten & Aquarium

Built in 1842, the Berlin Zoo is one of the world's oldest. It's also one of its smallest. Cages can be on the tiny side, but the work being done with endangered species is impressive. ⓐ Hardenbergplatz 8 ⓣ (030) 254 010 ⓦ www.zoo-berlin.de ⓛ 09.00–19.00 Mar–Aug; 09.00–18.00 Sept & Oct; 09.00–17.00 Nov–Feb ⓝ U-Bahn/S-Bahn: Zoologischer Garten. Admission charge

CULTURE

Bauhaus Archiv

This single-storey museum chronicles the output of the prolific Bauhaus design movement. The building was designed by the founder of the movement, Walter Gropius. ⓐ Klingelhöferstrasse 13–14 ⓣ (030) 254 0020 ⓦ www.bauhaus.de ⓛ 10.00–17.00 Wed–Mon ⓝ U-Bahn: Nollendorfplatz. Admission charge

Beate Uhse Erotik Museum

The inspirational Beate Uhse was a former Luftwaffe pilot and potato picker who made her millions selling marital aids and naughty videos. Over her lifetime she collected a heap of historical erotic artefacts, which are now exhibited in this museum located above her flagship sex shop. ⓐ Joachimstaler Str. 4 ⓣ (030) 886 0666 ⓦ www.erotikmuseum.de ⓛ 09.00–20.00 Mon–Sat, 11.00–00.00 Sun ⓝ U-Bahn/S-Bahn: Zoologischer Garten. Admission charge ⓘ 18s and over only

Bröhan-Museum

This peaceful museum features the collection of businessman Karl Bröhan. Articles of interest include a plethora of art nouveau and art deco pieces, plus an array of paintings from 1890 to the beginning

○ *Take a journey through film history at the Filmmuseum*

of World War II. A series of paintings by Hans Baluschek chronicles the social life of the Weimar period in the run-up to the dark days of Nazism. ⓐ Schlosstrasse 1A ⓣ (030) 3269 0600 ⓦ www.broehan-museum.de ⓛ 10.00–18.00 Tues–Sun ⓝ U-Bahn: Richard-Wagner-Platz. Admission charge

Filmmuseum Berlin

German film from the dawn of celluloid to modern day is chronicled in this fascinating museum. The *Metropolis* exhibits and Marlene Dietrich artefacts are of particular interest. ⓐ Potsdamer Str. 2 ⓣ (030) 300 9030 ⓦ www.filmmuseum-berlin.de ⓛ 10.00–18.00 Tues & Wed, Fri–Sun, 10.00–20.00 Thur ⓝ U-Bahn/S-Bahn: Potsdamer Platz. Admission charge

Gemäldegalerie

Early European paintings are displayed, each separated into rooms according to region and period. Pieces range from the Middle Ages to the 18th century. Rembrandt fans will be particularly pleased by the selection of 20 masterpieces by the Dutch painter. ⓐ Matthäikirchplatz, off Sigismundstrasse ⓣ (030) 266 42 3040 ⓛ 10.00–18.00 Tues & Wed, Fri–Sun, 10.00–22.00 Thur Ⓜ U-Bahn/S-Bahn: Potsdamer Platz. Admission charge (free after 18.00 Thur)

Hamburger Bahnhof: Museum für Gegenwart

Located in an old train station, this is one of the biggest private collections of contemporary art in the world, with over 2,000 works by more than 150 artists. The permanent collection features works by the likes of Andy Warhol and Cy Twombly. ⓐ Invalidenstrasse 50 -51 ⓣ (030) 3978 3411 Ⓦ www.hamburgerbahnhof.de ⓛ 10.00–18.00 Tues–Fri, 11.00–20.00 Sat, 11.00–18.00 Sun Ⓜ U-Bahn/S-Bahn: Hauptbahnhof. Admission charge

Museum Berggruen: Picasso und Seine Zeit

Three floors of art dedicated to the works of Picasso, Klee and Matisse, along with a few pieces by Cézanne and Giacometti. ⓐ Schlosstrasse 1 ⓣ (030) 3269 5815 Ⓦ www.smb.spk-berlin.de ⓛ 10.00–18.00 Tues–Sun Ⓜ U-Bahn: Richard-Wagner-Platz. Admission charge

Neue Nationalgalerie

The Neue Nationalgalerie brings art into the 20th century with a wonderful collection of modern work heavy on German artists. The building, designed by Mies van der Rohe, can feel a little sparse – but acts as a wonderful backdrop for art on display. ⓐ Potsdamer Str. 50 ⓣ (030) 266 2651 Ⓦ www.smb.spk-berlin.de ⓛ 10.00–18.00 Tues & Wed, Fri, 10.00–22.00 Thur, 11.00–18.00 Sat & Sun Ⓜ U-Bahn/S-Bahn: Potsdamer Platz. Admission charge

RETAIL THERAPY

Before reunification, Kurfürstendamm – or 'Ku'damm', as it is known by locals – was the height of chic. Here is where locals would find the designer boutiques, chain stores and flashing lights of urban living. When the Wall came down, East Berliners flocked here to see if the street really was paved with gold (it wasn't). No longer as trendy as it once was, it still puts up a good fight and can be heaving on the weekend, when gaggles of teenagers move from shop to shop. Meanwhile, Potsdamer Platz has finally completed its reconstruction and emerged as Berlin's favourite shopping mall. Glass and concrete provide the temperature-controlled environments so beloved by today's urban dwellers.

Books in Berlin Berlin's largest resource for English-language books. Everything from fiction to fact is available, including the usual bestsellers and classic novels. Don't go looking for anything too obscure. Special orders can be made for rarities and hard-to-finds. ⓐ Goethestrasse 69 ⓣ (030) 313 1233 ⓦ www.booksinberlin.de ⓛ 12.00–17.00 Mon–Fri, 10.00–16.00 Sat ⓝ S-Bahn: Savignyplatz

Budapester Schuhe Serious footwear fans will love this shop. Labels include Miu Miu, Dolce & Gabbana and JP Tod's. Selection tends to be on the conservative side, but all are of extremely high quality. An outlet store located at Bleibtreustrasse 24 holds out-of-season stock at prices slashed by as much as 50 per cent off the regular price. ⓐ Kurfürstendamm 43 ⓣ (030) 8862 4206 ⓦ www.budapester.eu ⓛ 10.00–19.00 Mon–Fri, 10.00–18.00 Sat ⓝ U-Bahn: Uhlandstrasse

Harvey's Cutting-edge men's fashion with a strong focus on Japanese designers like Issey Miyake and Yohji Yamamoto. Prices aren't outrageous considering what's on offer, but if you want to shop here you should be prepared to splash out. ⓐ Kurfürstendamm 55–56 ⓣ (030) 883 3803 ⓦ www.harveys-berlin.de ⓛ 11.00–20.00 Mon–Fri, 11.00–19.00 Sat ⓝ U-Bahn: Uhlandstrasse

Jil Sander Germany's biggest contribution to the world of haute couture may now be owned by Prada, but that doesn't stop the label from being one of the most popular in the country. ⓐ Kurfürstendamm 185 ⓣ (030) 886 7020 ⓦ www.jilsander.com ⓛ 10.00–19.00 Mon–Fri, 10.00–18.00 Sat ⓝ U-Bahn: Adenauerplatz

Ka De We Berlin's most famous department store, Ka De We is the city's Harrods, complete with a glorious food hall on the fifth floor.

● *Ka De We (Kaufhaus des Westens) is a shopper's paradise*

A good place to buy basics, including underwear, luggage and toiletries.
ⓐ Tauentzienstrasse 21–24 ☎ (030) 21210 ⓦ www.kadewe-berlin.de
🕐 10.00–20.00 Mon–Thur, 10.00–21.00 Fri, 09.30–20.00 Sat
Ⓝ U-Bahn: Wittenbergplatz

Peek & Cloppenburg While the ground floor is basics, and upstairs
is glamour, hit the basement for the big names of street fashion.
From Diesel to Tommy Hilfiger and Mavi Jeans, this is Berlin's
funkiest department store. ⓐ Tauentzienstrasse 19 ☎ (030) 212 900
🕐 10.00–20.00 Mon–Sat Ⓝ U-Bahn: Wittenbergplatz

Planet Going clubbing but haven't got a thing to wear? Planet
specialises in solving your party wardrobe crisis with its array of
lamé, leather and latex wear, perfect for any outrageous occasion.
ⓐ Schlüterstrasse 35 ☎ (030) 885 2717 ⓦ www.planetwear.de
🕐 11.30–19.30 Mon–Fri, 11.00–18.00 Sat Ⓝ U-Bahn: Savignyplatz

Stilwerk If you love IKEA but are looking for something a bit more
original, then Stilwerk may have what you need. Home furnishings,
lighting fixtures, interiors and kitchenware are jumbled into one
massive and convenient location. ⓐ Kantstrasse 17 ☎ (030) 315 150
ⓦ www.stilwerk.de 🕐 10.00–19.00 Mon–Sat Ⓝ S-Bahn: Savignyplatz

TAKING A BREAK

Café Hardenberg £ ❶ Food is simple, yet decent, including salads,
pastas and sandwiches, and the student clientele is a bonus.
ⓐ Hardenbergstrasse 10 ☎ (030) 312 2644 ⓦ www.cafehardenberg.de
🕐 09.00–01.00 Ⓝ U-Bahn: Ernst-Reuter-Platz

Café am Neuen See £–££ ② If a day wandering through Tiergarten is part of your plans, then be sure to include a stop at this peaceful café next to leafy Tiergarten lake. Coffee, cakes, light meals and fresh juices are available to enjoy on-site. ⓐ Lichtensteinallee 2 ① (030) 254 4930 ⓛ 10.00–02.00 (indoor seating only in winter) ⓝ S-Bahn: Tiergarten

Schwarzes Café £–££ ③ This 'open all hours' café draws the strangest mix of people. At various times throughout the day you will find yummy mummies, anarchist marchers and black-clad artists. ⓐ Kantstrasse 148 ① (030) 313 8038 ⓦ www.schwarzescafe-berlin.de ⓛ 24 hrs ⓝ S-Bahn: Savignyplatz

Café Einstein Stammhaus ££–£££ ④ Viennese-style coffee house complete with waiters in bow ties. International papers are available to read free of charge. Enjoy a rest while nibbling at the delicious apple strudel. In summer, breakfast is served in the garden.

● *Take a break in the Tiergarten – Berlin's green heart*

ⓐ Kurfürstenstrasse 58 ⓣ (030) 261 5096 ⓦ www.cafeeinstein.com
ⓛ 08.00–00.00 ⓝ U-Bahn: Nollendorfplatz

AFTER DARK

RESTAURANTS

Diener £ ❺ Probably the closest you will ever feel to living during the heady days of the Weimar Republic. This old-style bar features fading pictures of unknown Germans on the walls and dust-covered hunting murals. Choose something typically German from the menu to soak up the beer. ⓐ Grolmanstrasse 47 ⓣ (030) 881 5329 ⓦ www.diener-tattersall.de ⓛ 18.00–late ⓝ S-Bahn: Savignyplatz

Sachiko Sushi £–££ ❻ Berlin's only sushi bar with a revolving trolley. All of the dishes on offer are absolutely scrumptious. ⓐ Grolmanstrasse 47 ⓣ (030) 313 2282 ⓦ www.sachikosushi.com ⓛ 12.00–00.00 Mon–Sat, 16.00–00.00 Sun ⓝ S-Bahn: Savignyplatz

Edd's ££ ❼ Bookings are essential at the tasty Thai joint run by a fast and friendly husband-and-wife team. Dishes tend to be on the spicy side. No credit cards accepted. ⓐ Lützowstrasse 81 ⓣ (030) 215 5294 ⓦ www.edds-thairestaurant.de ⓛ 11.30–15.00, 18.00–00.00 Tues–Fri, 17.00–00.00 Sat, 14.00–00.00 Sun ⓝ U-Bahn: Kurfürstenstrasse

Julep's ££ ❽ Original American dishes that fuse traditional items such as nachos and burgers with more fusion sensibilities. The Caesar salad and rich chocolate brownies would make any Yankee homesick. ⓐ Giesebrechtstrasse 3 ⓣ (030) 881 8823 ⓦ www.juleps.de ⓛ 17.00–01.00 Mon–Wed & Sun, 17.00–02.00 Thur–Sat ⓝ U-Bahn: Adenauerplatz

Marjellchen ££ ❾ Specialities from East Prussia, Pomerania and Silesia. Russia may control its borders, but nothing will ever control the owner's desire to break out into song or recite poetry. ⓐ Mommsenstrasse 9 ⓣ (030) 883 2676 ⓦ www.marjellchen-berlin.de ⓛ 17.00–00.00 ⓝ S-Bahn: Savignyplatz

Florian ££–£££ ❿ Fab South German food and good staff make the place perpetually full. Dress up if you don't want to be shoved in a table near the toilets. ⓐ Grolmanstrasse 52 ⓣ (030) 313 9184 ⓦ www.restaurant-florian.de ⓛ 18.00–03.00 ⓝ S-Bahn: Savignyplatz

Paris Bar ££–£££ ⓫ French food in an atmosphere that makes you feel like you've just stepped off the Champs-Elysées. Art drips from every corner and you fully expect the cast of the Moulin Rouge to cancan in at any moment. ⓐ Kantstrasse 152 ⓣ (030) 313 8052 ⓦ www.parisbar.net ⓛ 12.00–late ⓝ S-Bahn: Savignyplatz

Hugo's £££ ⓬ Berlin's most award-winning restaurant combines classic and modern takes on favourite German dishes. As the restaurant is situated on the rooftop of the Intercontinental Hotel, the views are as inspiring as the food. ⓐ Intercontinental Hotel, Budapester Str. 2 ⓣ (030) 2602 1263 ⓦ www.hugos-restaurant.de ⓛ 18.00–22.00 Mon–Sat ⓝ U-Bahn/S-Bahn: Zoologischer Garten

BARS, CLUBS & DISCOS

A-Trane The programme at this tiny club features some of the finest modern jazz musicians around: such greats as Herbie Hancock, Wynton Marsalis and Diana Krall have graced the stage. ⓐ Bleibtreustrasse 1 ⓣ (030) 313 2550 ⓦ www.a-trane.de ⓛ 21.00–02.00 Sun–Thur, 21.00–late Fri & Sat ⓝ U-Bahn: Savignyplatz. Admission charge Sat until 00.30

Cotton Club With its unpretentious interior plastered in old jazz posters, the Cotton Club is a great place to dance to Latin grooves and lively jazz on a Saturday night. There's occasionally live music. ⓐ Carmerstrasse 2 ⓣ (030) 3644 1544 ⓦ www.cottonclubberlin.de ⓛ 20.00–late Mon–Sat ⓝ U-Bahn: Savignyplatz. Admission charge

Gainsbourg This popular American bar was named after the French singer-songwriter Serge Gainsbourg, and features one of the most comprehensive drinks menus in Berlin. ⓐ Savignyplatz 5 ⓣ (030) 313 7464 ⓦ www.gainsbourg.de ⓛ 17.00–late ⓝ S-Bahn: Savignyplatz

Victoria Bar Funky cocktail bar aimed at a relaxed crowd. The long bar, efficiently run by trained mixologists, draws the crowds in. The subdued lighting, muffled funk and restrained colours helps to keep them there. ⓐ Potsdamer Str. 102 ⓣ (030) 2575 9977 ⓦ www.victoriabar.de ⓛ 18.30–03.00 Sun–Thur, 18.30–04.00 Fri & Sat ⓝ U-Bahn: Kurfürstenstrasse

Vienna Bar This stylish bar boasts over 120 varieties of wine and champagne, and a creative brasserie menu to match. Go for the Wagyu beef house-burger. ⓐ Kantstrasse 152 ⓣ (030) 3101 5090 ⓦ www.vienna-bar.de ⓛ 17.00–late Tues–Sat ⓝ U-Bahn: Uhlandstrasse

CINEMAS & THEATRES

Arsenal The leading art film house in Berlin. Programming here is a mixed bag of everything from classic Hollywood to cutting-edge contemporary. ⓐ Potsdamer Str. 2 ⓣ (030) 2695 5100 ⓦ www.arsenal-berlin.de ⓝ U-Bahn/S-Bahn: Potsdamer Platz

CinemaxX Potsdamer Platz This multiplex is the biggest in town, with 19 screens to choose from – two or three of which usually show

something in English. Programming is strictly Hollywood blockbuster.
ⓐ Potsdamer Str. 5 ⓣ 01805 2463 6299 Ⓦ www.cinemaxx.de
Ⓝ U-Bahn/S-Bahn: Potsdamer Platz

Deutsche Oper Monolithic, 1,900-seat opera hall that plays
second fiddle to the grander and more centrally located Staatsoper.
ⓐ Bismarckstrasse 35 ⓣ (030) 343 8401 Ⓦ www.deutscheoperberlin.de
Ⓛ Box office: 11.00–18.00 Mon–Sat, 10.00–14.00 Sun Ⓝ U-Bahn:
Deustche Oper

Philharmonie Home to the world-renowned Berlin Philharmonic
Orchestra, the Philharmonie is probably the most difficult place for which
to snag a ticket. The music that emanates from this place is sublime,
especially under the artistic direction of conductor Sir Simon Rattle.
ⓐ Herbert-von-Karajan-Strasse 1 ⓣ (030) 2548 8999 Ⓦ www.berliner-
philharmoniker.de Ⓛ Box office: 15.00–18.00 Mon–Fri, 11.00–14.00
Sat & Sun Ⓝ U-Bahn/S-Bahn: Potsdamer Platz

Schaubühne am Leihniner Platz The who's who of young, cutting-
edge theatre flock here. ⓐ Kurfürstendamm 153 ⓣ (030) 890 023
Ⓦ www.schaubuehne.de Ⓛ Box office: 11.00–18.30 Mon–Sat,
15.00–18.30 Sun Ⓝ U-Bahn: Adenauerplatz

Wintergarten Varieté Slick and professional cabaret in
a classy environment. ⓐ Potsdamer Str. 96 ⓣ (030) 250 0880
Ⓦ www.wintergarten-berlin.de Ⓛ Box office opens 4 hrs before
start of show, Wed–Sun Ⓝ U-Bahn: Kurfürstenstrasse

▶ *The Orangery at Sanssouci, Potsdam*

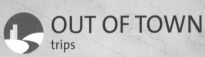

OUT OF TOWN
trips

Sachsenhausen

Sachsenhausen is a district of Oranienburg that contains a former concentration camp with the same name.

The camp was reopened one last time on 23 April 1961 as a national memorial, with a museum and memorial hall/cinema chronicling its devastating past. They can be found at either end of the parade ground, where prisoners were forced to watch executions on the gallows.

A GRIM REMINDER

The closest concentration camp to the city of Berlin, Sachsenhausen was opened in 1936 and used mainly as a holding pen for political prisoners and Communist sympathisers. Changes in policy meant that 6,000 Jews were shipped here immediately following Kristallnacht. By 1945, this number had increased to 33,000 prisoners.

Near the end of the war, as the Russians approached the city, all of the prisoners were marched to the Baltic Sea. They were then loaded onto ships which were sunk in order to hide traces of their existence. Sachsenhausen was liberated on 22 April 1945, and the only survivors were the 3,000 or so 'lucky ones' found in the camp hospital who were physically or mentally unable to embark on the trek.

Unfortunately, Sachsenhausen's status as a political detention camp and centre for mass killing didn't end when World War II was won. The Russian secret police reopened Sachsenhausen and gave it the title of Camp 7. After the fall of the GDR government, a mass grave of over 10,000 bodies was found on the grounds.

○ *The gates of Sachsenhausen concentration camp*

Next to the cinema is a prison and the bleak remains of the Station Z extermination block. A map allows visitors to trace the path of new arrivals, whether they were to be killed or used as slave labour. Despite the enlightened Germany of today, a few people have still tried to forget the past: in 1992, some of the buildings were destroyed by locals. Hire an English audio guide, as all the labels are in German only.

Gedenkstätte & Museum Sachsenhausen ❸ Strasse der Nationen 22, Oranienbuurg ❶ (0331) 200 200 ⓦ www.gedenkstaette-sachsen hausen.de ❺ 08.30–18.00 Tues–Sun, mid-Mar–mid-Oct; 08.30–16.30 Tues–Sun, mid-Oct–mid-Mar ⓢ S-Bahn: Oranienburg

GETTING THERE

Oranienburg is located at the end of the S1 S-Bahn line. From Mitte, the journey takes approximately 40 minutes. Follow the signs to Gedenkstätte Sachsenhausen after leaving the station. The walk should take about 20 minutes.

Potsdam

The capital of Brandenburg, Potsdam is Berlin's Versailles – a collection of stunning royal palaces, residences and parks that recall a time when the Prussian Empire ruled much of Central Europe.

Summer weekends draw huge crowds to Park Sanssouci (see page 126), which boasts a wonderful collection of palaces and buildings in the baroque style, notably the Schloss Sanssouci. For other great examples, check out the homes on Gutenberg Strasse and Brandenburger Strasse, the city's main pedestrianised shopping street. Three of the baroque town gates – the Brandenburger Tor, Jäger Tor and the Nauener Tor – still stand, and you can find them located on the northern and western sides of the district. The Brandenburger Tor, while not as famous as its Berlin-based namesake, is actually older by 18 years.

The Old Town suffered particularly in World War II. All that remains of the past in the main square are the Altes Rathaus (Old Town Hall, see page 124) and Nikolaikirche (see page 126). To get an idea of how the square looked prior to World War II, take a look at the model located in the lobby of the Altes Rathaus. The city's royal associations caused the GDR government to give it a wide berth and very little restoration was undertaken in the post-war years. In many ways this benefited the region as it meant that the palace didn't have to endure a typically botched East German patch-up job. All this changed in 1990, when UNESCO granted large areas of the city World Heritage Site status. Most of the original buildings have been restored and are as good as new.

GETTING THERE

Potsdam can be reached using public transport, as it is the terminus of the S1 S-Bahn. The journey time is just under an hour from Mitte.

Be sure to purchase a ticket that covers the 'C' zone or you will face a hefty fine. Regional trains leaving from Berlin's main train station are faster, but leave less frequently. Expect a journey time of 20–30 minutes.

SIGHTS & ATTRACTIONS

Altes Rathaus

Potsdam's old city hall was built in the mid-18th century. The tower was used as a prison until 1875. Today, the structure is used for ceremonies, lectures and exhibitions. ⓐ Am Alten Markt ⓣ (0331) 289 6336 ⓦ www.altesrathauspotsdam.de ⓘ Undergoing renovation work until 2012; call for updates

Biosphäre Potsdam

If you've ever been curious to find out what a coffee or cacao tree looks like, then head over to Potsdam's impressive living nature museum. With over 22,000 species in the collection, it's easy to spend an afternoon wandering through the tropical hot-houses amongst the orchids, ferns and venus fly-traps. ⓐ Georg-Hermann-Allee 99 ⓣ (0331) 550 740 ⓦ www.biosphaere-potsdam.net ⓛ 09.00–18.00 Mon–Fri, 10.00–19.00 Sat & Sun (last entry is 90 mins before closing time) ⓜ Tram: 96 to Buga-Park. Admission charge

Filmpark Babelsberg

A movie theme park that kids will love: it offers an action-packed stunt show, animal show, 4D cinema (where you experience wind and fog) and sets from the Wild West to the Middle Ages. Quentin Tarantino shot *Inglourious Basterds* at Studio Babelsberg next door. ⓐ Grossbeerenstrasse, Babelsberg, one S-Bahn stop east of Potsdam

STORY OF TWO CHURCHES

In its heyday, Potsdam was considered extremely cosmopolitan, and two churches act as testimonials to its forward-thinking approach. In 1685, the Great Elector promised refuge to protestants suffering from religious persecution in their homelands. It was a calculated move – and it worked incredibly well. The region suffered from a backwards reputation and it needed the brains, brawn and financial bonuses that a population boom could give them in order to play along with Europe's big boys. The Französische Kirche was built to accommodate the waves of Huguenots that descended on Potsdam, while St Peter's and St Paul's was constructed for Catholic immigrants who moved to the city in order to cash in on the new demands for skilled workers and soldiers.

ⓣ (0331) 721 2750 **ⓦ** www.filmpark-babelsberg.de **ⓛ** 10.00–18.00 Tues–Sun, Apr–Oct **ⓢ** S-Bahn: Babelsberg, then bus: 690. Admission charge

Gedenkstätte Lindenstrasse

The East German police once used these cells for interrogation, and the complex still feels decidedly eerie, even though the Stasi are now consigned to the past. **ⓐ** Lindenstrasse 54 **ⓣ** (0331) 289 6136 **ⓛ** 09.00–18.00 Tues–Sat

Haus der Brandenburgisch-Preussischen Geschichte

Formerly the royal stables, this house chronicles 800 years of Brandenburg history. **ⓐ** Kutschstall, Am Neuen Markt 9

① (0331) 620 8550 **Ⓦ** www.hbpg.de **🕔** 10.00–17.00 Tues–Fri,
10.00–18.00 Sat & Sun. Admission charge

Jan Bouman Haus

In an effort to draw Dutch settlers to Germany, the King built
134 gable-fronted houses in Potsdam. The scheme failed miserably.
At the time, the Netherlands was an economic, social and cultural
powerhouse while Germany was backwards, dirty and suffered
miserably from disease and pestilence. A few came, though, and this
house shows what life would have been like for them. **ⓐ** Mittelstrasse 8
① (0331) 280 3773 **Ⓦ** www.jan-bouman-haus.de **🕔** 13.00–18.00 Mon–Fri,
11.00–18.00 Sat & Sun. Admission charge

Marmorpalais

This neoclassical palace was the home of King Friedrich Wilhelm II.
ⓐ Im Neuen Garten **①** (0331) 969 4550 **Ⓦ** www.spsg.de **🕔** 10.00–18.00
Tues–Sun, May–Oct; 10.00–16.00 Sat & Sun, Nov–Apr; guided tours
Nov–Apr only. Admission charge

Nikolaikirche

This large church, built in the 19th century, dominates the old
town due to its large dome. The dome is said to have been built to
resemble St Paul's in London. **ⓐ** Am Alten Markt **①** (0331) 270 8602
Ⓦ www.nikolaipotsdam.de **🕔** 10.00–17.00 Mon–Sat, 11.30–17.00 Sun.
Admission charge for tower

Sanssouci

Absolutely stunning at all times, Park Sanssouci houses a collection
of palaces both big and small. Despite its large size, summer days
can see the wide avenues heaving with tourists and some of the

larger palaces become difficult to enter, as guided tours are compulsory. If the tours sell out (as they often do) then there will be very little chance of you going inside.

The park was built under the orders of King Frederick the Great, who fell in love with the area's inspiring views. His original plans saw the creation of a series of terraced gardens, but a desire to enjoy the peacefulness of the region caused him to add a palace. The name 'Sanssouci' was carefully chosen by the king to reflect the nature of the palace and what it meant to him (translated from the French, it means 'without a care'). The original palace is semi-circular in shape and located at the top of a terrace. While it was once a fully operational home for royals, it now houses a collection of paintings.

🔺 *Sanssouci – Berlin's Versailles*

Following victory in the Seven Years' War, the king decided to add another palace to the complex in the form of the Neues Palais on the park's western edge. Among the rooms worthy of exploration are the Marmorsaal (Marble Room), Grottensaal (Grotto Room), Schlosstheater (Palace Theatre) and Friedrich II's luxurious suite.

If interiors don't float your boat, or the crowds bar you from going inside, there is still plenty to see in the park grounds. Some of the more intriguing finds are the Chinesisches Teehaus (Chinese Teahouse), with its collection of Chinese and Meissen porcelain, the Drachenhaus (Dragonhouse) café built to resemble a pagoda, the Orangery and the incredible Spielfestung – a toy fortress built for the sons of Wilhelm II complete with a toy cannon which could be fired.

Go to the park's southwest corner to check out the Schloss Charlottenhof. Featuring a blue-glaze entrance and fascinating

🔺 *The formal gardens at Sanssouci*

BEYOND SANSSOUCI

Outside the park and old town there are even more sights to see. Fans of engineering will be intrigued by the Dampfmaschinenhaus on Breite Strasse. This building, built to look like a mosque, served to pump millions of gallons of water into Park Sanssouci for its fountains.

Another large park complex lies to the northeast of the town centre in the form of the Neuer Garten. Friedrich Wilhelm II, nephew to Fredrick the Great and successor to the throne, ordered the construction of these gardens in order to have a private green space available away from prying eyes. His lifestyle was famously outrageous – and he died young as a result of his self-indulgence.

Last, but not least, is Potsdam's third and most recently constructed royal park, Park Babelsberg. In East German times, it fell into disrepair due to its proximity to the border. If you think you are seeing Windsor Castle during your walk through the grounds, don't be shocked. Schloss Babelsberg, built among the park's wooden slopes, was inspired by the British royal residence.

Other oddities include the Flawoturm, an observation point constructed in mock medieval style close to the Glienicker See, and the Einsteinturm, designed by Erich Mendelsohn in 1921 in the expressionist style. The purpose of this building was to house an observatory that could confirm Einstein's theory of relativity. What makes this building so intriguing is that it acts as a symbol of the wit and whimsy that existed during the inter-war years when a true avant-garde movement existed.

Kupferstichzimmer (copper-plate engraving room), the palace
was built for Crown Prince Friedrich Wilhelm IV in the 1830s.
ⓐ Maulbeerallee ⓣ (0331) 969 4200 ⓦ www.spsg.de ⓛ Palace &
exhibition buildings: 10.00–18.00 Tues–Sun, Apr–Oct; 10.00–17.00
Tues–Sun, Nov–Mar; park: 09.00–dusk. Admission charge for
palace & exhibitions

Schloss Cecilienhof

Located in Park Sanssouci's northern corner, the Schloss Cecilienhof
was the last royal palace to be built in Potsdam. The mock-Tudor
mansion was built for the Kaiser's son and his wife. World War II buffs
may recognise the building from pictures of the Potsdam conference,
for it was within these walls that Churchill, Stalin and Truman met
to carve up Germany. ⓐ Im Neuen Garten ⓣ (0331) 969 4200
ⓦ www.spsg.de ⓛ 10.00–18.00 Tues–Sun, Apr–Oct; 10.00–17.00
Tues–Sun, Nov–Mar. Admission charge for palace

CULTURE

Filmmuseum Potsdam

A permanent exhibition exploring the output of the Babelsberg
studios. Special focus is placed on the films produced during the time
of the East German government. ⓐ Breite Str. 1a ⓣ (0331) 271 8112
ⓦ www.filmmuseum-potsdam.de ⓛ 10.00–18.00 Tues–Sun.
Admission charge

TAKING A BREAK

Waschbar £ ❶ Loved by locals, the Waschbar is a baffling mix of
café, bar, live music venue and… laundromat. Great for baguettes

and burgers, it's a relaxed place to re-fuel after wandering around Sanssouci. ⓐ Geschwister-Scholl-Str. 82 ⓣ (0331) 967 8716 ⓦ www.waschbar-pdm.de ⓛ 10.00–00.00

Café Heider £–££ ❷ Known more for its coffees and cakes, this café is also a cosy place to enjoy a filling meal. Nothing much to rave about taste-wise – it's more a place to experience friendly, fast service and fill yourself up. ⓐ Friedrich-Ebert-Strasse 29 ⓣ (0331) 270 5596 ⓦ www.cafeheider.de ⓛ 08.00–00.00 Mon–Fri, 09.00–late Sat, 10.00–late Sun

AFTER DARK

RESTAURANTS
Matschkes Galerie Café £ ❸ Simple German and Russian food that's heavy on taste (and stodge). You'd better love a good dumpling if you want to savour a night here. Outdoor courtyard seating makes summer dining delicious. ⓐ Alleestrasse 10 ⓣ (0331) 280 0359 ⓦ www.matschkes-galeriecafe.de ⓛ 12.00–23.00 Tues–Sun

Massimo 18 ££ ❹ This Italian eatery in a fine old townhouse makes a nice change from German restaurants – and the views over Schloss Cecilienhof and Marmorpalais are magnificent. ⓐ Mittelstrasse 18 ⓣ (0331) 8171 8983 ⓦ www.massimo18.de ⓛ 12.00–00.00

BARS & CLUBS
Bar Gelb This cosy bar is a good choice for pre-party drinks. With an extensive cocktail list, both alcoholic and non-alcoholic, it has something for everyone. ⓐ Dortustrasse 6 ⓣ (0331) 8871 5575 ⓦ www.bargelb.com ⓛ 08.00–02.00

Lindenpark Regular club nights and gigs in Babelsberg. Good for a solid night out on the town. ⓐ Stahnsdorfer Str. 76–78 ⓣ (0331) 747 970 ⓦ www.lindenpark.de ⓛ Hours vary: check website. Admission charge

Waschhaus DJs and live musicians get the crowd going at this large club located just outside the centre of Potsdam. Check the website for programme details as opening times vary. ⓐ Schiffbauergasse 6 ⓣ (0331) 271 560 ⓦ www.waschhaus.de. Admission charge

● *Wood-clad houses in the Russian colony of Alexandrowka*

ALEXANDROWKA

A 15-minute walk north of Potsdam centre takes you to probably the strangest sight in the region. A Russian colony was built here in 1826 by Friedrich Wilhelm III to commemorate the death of Tsar Alexander I. Thirteen wooden-clad, two-storey dwellings were built, each with steeply pitched roofs laid out in the shape of a St Andrew's Cross. The onion-domed church that rises behind the houses will make you feel like you're somewhere in the Urals.

The settlement became home to the members of a Russian troupe of musicians given into Prussian military service by the Tsar in 1812, and two of the houses are still inhabited by their descendants. Following World War II, the Soviets moved in. Villas to the north of the colony served as offices for the Soviet administration or as officers' homes. As Potsdam's highest observation point, Alexandrowka fell into disuse after the Wall went up in 1961 as locals were also banned from enjoying views over West Berlin.

THEATRE & LIVE MUSIC

Theaterschiff Potsdam Floating cabaret on a boat/theatre that the artists built themselves. Typical offerings include live performance, theatre, live bands, dance and cabaret, and every Saturday it's disco night from 23.00 until late. Check the website for programme details. ❸ Alte Fahrt ❶ (0331) 280 0100 ❿ www.theaterschiff-potsdam.de ❹ 17.00–01.00 Tues–Sun (closes later on Sat). Admission charge

Leipzig

East Germany's second city fell to ruin under the beleaguered leadership of the GDR government. Investment and Western business is now helping the city battle back from its smog-filled past, but there's still some work left to do.

Leipzig has long been considered a centre for education and culture; indeed it was here that the seeds of rebellion against Soviet control were first sown. Trade fairs are what bring the masses here now, with shows dedicated to everything from toys to books. The shows pack city hotels for weeks of schmoozing every year. In fact, it was at the 1902 Leipzig toy fair that a small stuffed bear was exhibited to the world by the Steiff toy company, sparking the international craze for the teddy bear.

Leipzig is an easy city to get to and navigate. The city centre is extremely compact and is focused around the buzz of Markt, the old market square. Here is where you will find the Old Town Hall, Königshaus and Town Museum: for details of all three, contact the tourist office on ❶ (0341) 710 4265.

Immediately behind the **Altes Rathaus** (Old Town Hall ❷ Markt ❶ (0341) 261 7760 ❸ 10.00–18.00 Tues–Sun), is the Old Stock Exchange, built in 1687. You'll spot it by the statue of its favourite son and noted academic, Goethe, in front of its quaint doors. Mädler Passage is a beautiful shopping arcade worth checking out, if only to admire the architecture that houses the cute, crafty shops located inside.

South of Thomaskirche is the New Town Hall, ironically named since the site can be traced back to the 16th century. Other musts include the Museum der Bildenden Künste Leipzig (Museum of Arts Picture Gallery Leipzig) for its collection of Old Masters, the Egyptian

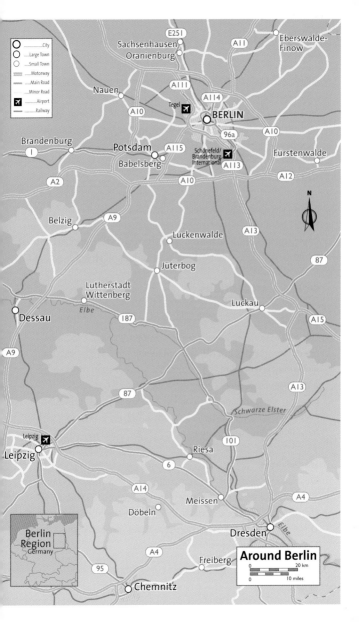

treasures of Leipzig University (whose alumni include Wagner, Schumann and the aforementioned Goethe) and the fascinating Museum in der 'Runde Ecke', with its displays of all things Stasi, including jars that collected the scent and body odour of suspected enemies of the state.

GETTING THERE

Leipzig is located 130 km (81 miles) southwest of Berlin. Direct trains depart from the central train station approximately every two hours. Rapid services are scheduled during the rush hour from Ostbahnhof, which cuts the journey time down by about half an hour.

SIGHTS & ATTRACTIONS

Leipzig Zoo

Like most European zoos, space is cramped. Some of the cages are downright sad, but it's a potential place to take the kids for a morning if you want to see something other than churches and museums. ⓐ Pfaffendorfer Str. 29 ⓣ (0341) 593 3500 ⓦ www.zoo-leipzig.de ⓛ 09.00–19.00, May–Sept; 09.00–18.00 Mon–Fri, 09.00–19.00 Sat & Sun, Apr & Oct; 09.00–17.00, Nov–Mar. Admission charge

Nikolaikirche

This baroque church played a solid role in the downfall of Communism. Free-speech meetings began here in 1982, eventually leading to the formation of the 'Swords to Ploughshares' peace movement. ⓐ Nikolaikirchhof 3 ⓣ (0341) 960 5270 ⓦ www.nikolaikirche-leipzig.de ⓛ Visits: 10.00–18.00; call for service times

Leipzig is an easy day trip from Berlin

BACH'S SECOND HOME

Just off the southwest corner of Markt is the Thomaskirche. This is famous for being the home of Johann Sebastian Bach for the 27 years he spent in the city as choirmaster of the Thomas' Boys Choir. Bach's grave is located in the chancel and a statue stands immediately outside the main entrance. For a view of Leipzig take a tour up to the church steeple. ⓐ Thomaskirchhof 18 ⓣ (0341) 222 24200 ⓦ www.thomaskirche.org ⓛ 09.00–18.00; steeple tours: 13.00, 14.00 & 16.30 Sat, 14.00 & 15.00 Sun. Admission charge for steeple tour

CULTURE

Bach-Museum

Just what you think it's going to be – an entire museum dedicated to Johann Sebastian Bach. Documents, instruments and furniture are just some of the items used to chronicle the composer's life and times. ⓐ Thomaskirchhof 13/14 ⓣ (0341) 913 7200 ⓦ www.bach-leipzig.de ⓛ 10.00–18.00 Tues–Sun. Admission charge

Grassi Museum für Angewandte Kunst

This museum is actually one of the oldest in the city, founded in 1874 to examine Applied Arts. The collection features textiles, ceramics, porcelain, furniture, glass, metal and sculpture. Entry is free on the first Wednesday of the month. ⓐ Johannisplatz 5–11 ⓣ (0341) 222 9100 ⓦ www.grassimuseum.de ⓛ 10.00–18.00 Tues–Sun. Admission charge

Museum der Bildenden Künste Leipzig

A splendid showcase for around 2,200 works of art. Treasures include 15th- and 16th-century German, Flemish and Dutch masters, expressionists and GDR creators. Look out for big names, including Rembrandt, Dürer and Rubens. ⓐ Katarienen Str. 10 ⓣ (0341) 216 990 ⓦ www.mdbk.de ⓛ 10.00–18.00 Tues, Thur–Sun, 12.00–20.00 Wed. Admission charge

Museum in der 'Runde Ecke'

The exhibition entitled 'Stasi: Power and Banality', is dedicated to the secret arts and methods of the feared secret police. Detailing its Soviet military origins and the scope of its power, it covers everything from the initial room of interrogation to Stasi disguises, bugs and the interception of letters. ⓐ Dittrichring 24 ⓣ (0341) 961 2443 ⓦ www.runde-ecke-leipzig.de ⓛ 10.00–18.00

Stadtgeschichtliches Museum

Informative museum discussing the history of Leipzig. Now housed inside the walls of the Renaissance Altes Rathaus (Old Town Hall). ⓐ Markt 1 ⓣ (0341) 965 1320 ⓦ www.stadtgeschichtliches-museum-leipzig.de ⓛ 10.00–18.00 Tues–Sun. Admission charge (under-16s free)

AFTER DARK

RESTAURANTS

Apels Garten £–££ Attractive German restaurant with a few dishes that are out of the ordinary. ⓐ Kolonnadenstrasse 2 ⓣ (0341) 960 7777 ⓦ www.apels-garten.de ⓛ 11.00–23.00 Mon–Sat, 11.00–15.30 Sun

Barthels Hof £–££ More delicious Saxon dishes in a cosy, panelled guesthouse. ⓐ Hainstrasse 1 ⓣ (0341) 141 310 ⓦ www.fantastic-restaurants.de ⓛ 19.00–00.00

🔺 *Sample classic Saxon fare at historic Auerbachs Keller*

Auerbachs Keller ££ Classic Saxon dishes including schnitzel, pork, dumplings and sauerkraut. ⓐ Mädlerpassage, Grimmaische Str. 2–4 ⓣ (0341) 216 100 ⓦ www.auerbachs-keller-leipzig.de ⓛ 11.30–00.00

El Matador ££ Decent Spanish food in a city not known for its foreign restaurants. For when you're all sausaged out. ⓐ Friedrich-Ebert-Strasse 108 ⓣ (0341) 980 0876 ⓛ 17.30–late Mon–Sat

BARS & CLUBS

Distillery As Leipzig is a University town, it has more than its fair share of clubbing hotspots. This is one of the best options to catch German and international DJs and live acts. ⓐ Kurt-Eisner-Strasse 4 ⓣ (0341) 3559 7400 ⓦ www.distillery.de ⓛ 23.30–late Fri, 23.00–late Sat. Admission charge

Ilses Erika Another atmospheric venue, this industrial bunker-esque basement features local and international live acts and DJs, playing alternative pop, techno, electro, house and soul. Check the website for programme details, as they do not have a phone. ⓐ Bernhard-Göring-Strasse 152 ⓣ (0341) 306 5111 ⓦ www.ilseserika.de. Admission charge

THEATRES & CONCERT HALLS

Moritzbastei Tucked behind the Gewandhaus Concert Hall, you'll find the Moritzbastei. Students began renovating this basement labyrinth back in the 1970s. Since reunification it's become a place for culture and music, hosting exhibitions, discussions and theatre, as well as a range of live music. ⓐ Universitätsstrasse 9 ⓣ (0341) 702 590 ⓦ www.moritzbastei.de. Admission charge

Gewandhaus zu Leipzig The Leipziger Gewandhaus Orchestra is one of the world's finest orchestras – and these brown, glass-fronted buildings are where you can listen to the magic. ⓐ Augustusplatz 8 ⓘ (0341) 127 0280 ⓦ www.gewandhaus.de ⓛ Box office: 10.00–18.00 Mon–Fri, 10.00–14.00 Sat

Opernhaus Leipzig Another performance venue with an excellent reputation in this city of multiple musicians. This venue focuses on opera. ⓐ Augustusplatz 12 ⓘ (0341) 126 1261 ⓦ www.oper-leipzig.de ⓛ Box office: 10.00–20.00 Mon–Fri, 10.00–18.00 Sat

ACCOMMODATION

Accento Hotel Leipzig £ Stylish hotel with efficient staff in a decent location. ⓐ Taucher Str. 260 ⓘ (0341) 92620 ⓦ www.precisehotels.com

Adagio Minotel Leipzig £–££ Central boutique hotel with individually designed rooms. ⓐ Seeburgstrasse 96 ⓘ (0341) 216 690 ⓦ www.hotel-adagio.de

Hotel Mercure Leipzig £–££ A little bland but the location can't be beaten. ⓐ Gutenbergplatz 1–5 ⓘ (0341) 12930 ⓦ www.mercure.com

Seaside Park Hotel ££–£££ A truly luxurious, art nouveau-style place to rest your head. ⓐ Richard-Wagner-Strasse 7 ⓘ (0341) 98520 ⓦ www.park-hotel-leipzig.de

---

ⓞ *Berlin has an excellent tram system*

PRACTICAL
information

Directory

GETTING THERE

By air

For most visitors, flying is the quickest and most convenient way to get to Berlin. The new Brandenburg International Airport (see page 48) will be the entry point for most scheduled flights when it replaces Tegel and Schönefeld Airports in 2011-2012. There are good public transport connections from all airports to the city centre.

Airlines flying direct to Berlin from London include: **Air Berlin** (W www.airberlin.com), **bmi** (W www.flybmi.com), **British Airways** (W www.britishairways.com), **Lufthansa** (W www.lufthansa.de) and **easyJet** (W www.easyjet.com). Those travelling from a regional airport may need to change planes. Travellers from the US currently need to make a transfer in a European hub, although a non-stop service from the US is expected to start once Brandenburg International is ready.

Many people are aware that air travel emits CO_2, which contributes to climate change. You may be interested in the possibility of lessening the environmental impact of your flight through **Climate Care** (W www.climatecare.org), which offsets your CO_2 by funding environmental projects around the world.

By rail

Though travelling by rail is often a more expensive option than flying from the UK, it at least allows you the chance to see something of the countryside. The most common routes cut through Belgium and into Germany via Cologne and Hanover.

There are fast and comfortable connections via France from London's St Pancras International station with Eurostar. This involves a change in Brussels or Calais. The total journey time is approximately 12–16 hours, depending on connections.

The monthly *Thomas Cook European Rail Timetable* has up-to-date schedules for European international and domestic train services.

Eurostar ⓣ +44 8432 186 186 ⓦ www.eurostar.com

Thomas Cook European Rail Timetable ⓣ +44 1733 416 477
ⓦ www.thomascookpublishing.com

By road

Long-distance buses connect Berlin with most other European countries. Travellers may have to change buses in Brussels to reach their final destination. From London, by **National Express**, the fastest journey time is 17–24 hours, depending on connections. See ⓦ www.nationalexpress.com.

If you want to drive, the German motorway system is well integrated in the European motorway network. The easiest motorway to use is the A2, which cuts across Germany and passes through Dortmund and Hannover from close to the Dutch border to terminate at Berlin. The trip from London via Calais, Bruges, Gent, Antwerp, Eidhoven, Dortmund and Hanover is, frankly, a bit dull and takes approximately 12 hours.

Driving in Berlin is comparable to the UK and US in terms of the wide, straight roads and clear signals. Congestion can sometimes be a problem, especially during rush hour.

If you choose to drive, do bear in mind some simple rules. Germans drive on the right-hand side of the road. When you approach a crossroads that doesn't have a traffic signal, drivers must yield to traffic from the right. The only exception to this rule is when the crossroads is marked by a diamond-shaped yellow sign. Trams always have right of way. An *einbahnstrasse* is a one-way street. Parking on side-streets is free but spaces are hard to find; on some busier streets, you may have to purchase a ticket from a nearby machine (expect to pay €1 per hour – most multi-storey and underground parking lots charge €2 per hour). If you park illegally, your car may be clamped or towed away.

ENTRY FORMALITIES

Visitors to Germany who are citizens of the UK, Ireland, Australia, the US, Canada or New Zealand will need a passport, but not a visa for stays of up to three months. South African nationals do require a visa. If you are travelling from other countries, you may need a visa; it is best to check before you leave home.

Visitors from outside the EU are subject to restrictions in what they can bring into the country. Tobacco limits (for persons over 17) are 200 cigarettes or 50 cigars or 250 grams of tobacco. Alcohol limits (for persons over 17) are 2 litres of wine or 1 litre of liquor or 16 litres of beer. Duty-free limits for those travelling from another EU country are higher – 800 cigarettes or 200 cigars of 1 kg of tobacco, and 90 litres of wine or 10 litres of spirits or 110 litres of beer.

Everything you bring into the country must be for personal use or a present and must not be for sale. When buying souvenirs, you should also consider the customs regulations of your home country.

As entry requirements and customs regulations are subject to change, you should always check the current situation with your local travel agent, airline or a German embassy or consulate before you leave. For up-to-date German customs information, see Ⓦ www.zoll.de.

MONEY

The currency in Germany is the euro. If you are coming from another country in the EU that uses the euro currency, you will not need to change money. A euro is divided into 100 cents. Euros come in notes of €5, €10, €20, €50, €100, €200 and €500. Coins are in denominations of €1 and €2, and in cents worth 1c, 2c, 5c, 10c, 20c and 50c.

The most widely accepted credit card is Mastercard. American Express and Visa are less commonly permitted. Many smaller businesses, including some restaurants, taverns, smaller hotels and most market stalls, do not accept credit card payment. This is especially true outside Berlin and the main tourist destinations. It is advisable always to carry a small amount of cash to cover your day's purchases.

HEALTH, SAFETY & CRIME

It is not necessary to take any special health precautions while travelling in Germany. Tap water is safe to drink. However, do not drink any water from surrounding lakes or rivers, as the region is not known for its commitment towards environmentalism. Many Germans prefer *Mineralwasser* (bottled mineral water).

Apotheken (Pharmacies) are marked by a large green cross. German pharmacists are always well stocked and staff can provide expert advice. EU residents who need to visit a doctor or dentist in an emergency should show a European Health Insurance Card (EHIC). This entitles holders to free or reduced-cost treatment, although you may have to pay upfront and arrange reimbursement when back in your home country. Keep all prescriptions, reports and receipts. It is advisable to have private travel insurance in addition to the card.

As in any other big cities, crime is a fact of life in Berlin. Petty theft (bag-snatching, pick-pocketing) is the most common form of trouble for tourists. However, you are unlikely to experience violence or assault. Never leave valuables lying openly in your car, and always lock it. When using public transport or walking on the street, carry your wallet in your front pocket, keep bags closed at all times, never leave valuables on the ground when you are seated at a table, and always wear camera bags and handbags crossed over your chest.

Strolling around the inner city at night is fairly safe, but avoid dimly lit streets. Some of the eastern neighbourhoods are still a little rough. If you plan on exploring the nightlife in these industrial districts, it is best to take a cab. Your hotel will warn you about particular areas to avoid.

OPENING HOURS

Most businesses open 09.00–18.30 Monday to Friday. Retail shops often stay open until 20.00. On Saturdays, smaller boutiques will close at 14.00, while larger department stores and chains extend hours to 20.00. Stores generally do not open on Sundays or public holidays (except for florists). Banks open 08.00–13.00, 14.00–16.00 Monday to Friday (until 15.30 on Thursdays).

⬤ *A communist-era mural on Karl Marx Allee*

Cultural institutions usually close for one day per week – usually Mondays. Standard hours are 09.00–18.00. Only the biggest and most popular sights remain open seven days a week.

Usual post office opening hours are 08.30–18.30 Monday to Friday, and 08.00–13.00 Saturday.

TOILETS

At airports, railway stations, U-Bahn and S-Bahn stations, you should not have a problem finding toilets although you may be charged between €0.50–€1.50 for the privilege. Germans are so obsessed with their bowel functions that many toilets even have a shelf installed to allow users to admire what they leave behind before they flush. Most locals, when pressed, resort to using facilities at cafés, restaurants and bars, though using them may not be appreciated if you are not a customer.

The cleanest public toilets are those with an attendant, who expects a small tip of around €0.50. Another good bet for a clean loo are the toilets at museums. Women's toilets are often marked with the usual pictograms, but if not, they will be marked with either 'D' for *Damen* or 'F' for *Frauen* (Ladies). 'H' means *Herren* (Gentlemen).

CHILDREN

Germany is generally a child-friendly place and no special health precautions need be taken for children. Most restaurants welcome children, some even having play corners or outdoor playgrounds. There is usually a kids' menu with smaller portions to go with the normal menu and, if you ask, the staff will often be able to supply your children with pencils and paper at the table.

Nappies and other baby articles are readily obtained from supermarkets, *Apotheken* (pharmacies) or a *Drogerie* – like a drugstore, but without prescription medications.

There are plenty of attractions in and around Berlin that will keep the kids occupied, but if the numerous museums and historic sights prove to be a little overwhelming, consider taking them to one of the many indoor playgrounds that have been built in converted industrial spaces. Inflatable mountains, air hockey tables and trampolines are just some of the activities children can enjoy. Top centres are:

Jacks Fun World ⓐ Miraustrasse 38 ⓣ (030) 4190 0242 ⓦ www.jacks-fun-world.de ⓛ 14.00–19.30 Tues–Fri, 10.00–20.00 Sat & Sun ⓝ S-Bahn: Eichborndamm. Admission charge

Jolos Kinderwelt ⓐ Am Tempelhofer Berg 7d ⓣ (030) 6120 2796 ⓦ www.jolo-berlin.de ⓛ 14.00–19.00 Mon–Fri, 11.00–19.00 Sat & Sun ⓝ U-Bahn: Platz der Luftbrücke. Admission charge

MACHmit! Museum für Kinder A hands-on museum crossed with a fun park. There are workshops, games and activities where the kids can get creative. And if they're bursting with energy, let them loose in the climbing labyrinth and the hall of mirrors. ⓐ Senefelderstrasse 5 ⓣ (030) 7477 8200 ⓦ www.machmitmuseum.de ⓛ 10.00–18.00 Tues–Sun ⓝ U-Bahn: Eberswalder Strasse. Admission charge

COMMUNICATIONS
Internet
Internet access is provided by some libraries and internet cafés around the city. One of the largest and most popular cafés is:
Sidewalk Express Internet Point While €2 per hour isn't the cheapest option, your ticket is valid for seven days and you can use it at any of the other Sidewalk Express locations around town. The most central is ⓐ Hardenbergerplatz 2 ⓣ (030) 2789 0301 ⓦ www.sidewalkexpress.com ⓛ 06.00–23.00 Sun–Thur, 06.00–00.00 Fri & Sat

TELEPHONING GERMANY

To call Berlin from abroad, dial the access code (00 from the UK, 011 from the US), followed by Germany's country code 49, followed by 30 for Berlin and then the local number. To call Berlin from within Germany, dial 030 and then the local number.

TELEPHONING ABROAD

When making an international call, dial 00, then the international code, then the area code dropping the initial zero, then the phone number you require. The international dialling code for calls from Germany to Australia is 61, to the UK 44, to the Irish Republic 353, to South Africa 27, to New Zealand 64, and to the USA and Canada 1.

Phone

Coin-operated public phones are rare; far more common are card-operated phones. *Telefonkarten* (telephone cards) can be bought at any post office and some shops such as bookshops or kiosks at railway stations.

If you intend to make a lot of calls while in Berlin, it might be a good idea to purchase a local SIM card for your mobile phone. If you wish to use your UK SIM card while abroad, make sure you have activated 'roaming' – and be aware that you will pay to receive calls as well as to make them.

Post

Postal services are quick and efficient and there are many offices throughout the city. The national service, Deutsche Post, is recognisable by the symbol of a black bugle on a yellow background. The most convenient locations can be found at the airport, main railway station and inside Friedrichstrasse station.

Stamps can be bought at the post offices or from automatic vending machines outside post offices. Post boxes are yellow.

ELECTRICITY

The standard electrical current is 220 volts. Two-pin adaptors can be purchased at most electrical shops.

TRAVELLERS WITH DISABILITIES

Facilities for visitors with disabilities are generally quite good in Germany. These facilities are usually indicated by a blue pictogram of a person in a wheelchair. In all towns and cities you'll find designated parking spaces for people with disabilities. Additionally, motorway service stops, airports and main railway stations always have suitable toilet facilities. Most trains also have toilets that are accessible for wheelchairs. Most cinemas, theatres, museums and public buildings are accessible. Many of Berlin's hotels are wheelchair-friendly but you will need to make a special request when you book.

There is a good section for visitors with disabilities on the tourist information website Ⓦ www.visitberlin.de – click 'Berlin for...' then 'Handicapped'. Other useful sources of advice when in Germany are:

Mobidat ⓐ Langhansstrasse 64, Berlin ⓣ (030) 7477 7115
Ⓦ www.mobidat.net ⓛ 08.00–17.00 Mon–Thur, 08.00–16.00 Fri

BSK – Bundesverbandes Selbsthilfe Körperbehinderter e.V.
ⓐ Altkrautheimer Str. 20, 74238 Krautheim ⓣ (06294) 4281 50
Ⓦ www.reisen-ohne-barrieren.eu

Barrierefreier Tourismus Info ⓐ Bergstrasse 45, Kaiserslautern
ⓣ (01803) 1424 3464 Ⓦ www.barrierefreier-tourismus.info

TOURIST INFORMATION

Before arriving in Berlin, check out the tourist information website
🌐 www.visitberlin.de, which has a host of useful information and
ideas. You can also call the hotline on 📞 (030) 250 025. Another
useful site is 🌐 www.berlin.de.

When you arrive, look out for BERLIN infostores, located in
various places across the city. These have maps, leaflets and English-
speaking consultants. The handiest are at:

Berlin Hauptbahnhof ⓐ Entrance to Europa Platz 🕐 08.00–22.00
🅝 U-Bahn/S-Bahn: Hauptbahnhof

Brandenburger Tor ⓐ Pariser Platz (south wing) 🕐 10.00–18.00
🅝 U-Bahn/S-Bahn: Brandenburger Tor

ALEXA shopping centre ⓐ Grunerstrasse 20 🕐 10.00–22.00
Mon–Sat, 11.00–16.00 Sun 🅝 U-Bahn/S-Bahn: Alexanderplatz

BACKGROUND READING

The Berlin Blockade by Ann & John Tusa. Gripping account of the
11 months when Berliners relied on air drops from Allied Forces to survive.
Berlin Game, Mexico Set, London Match by Len Deighton. Three classic
Cold War espionage thrillers using 1980s Berlin as a background.
The Berlin Wall by Norman Gelb. The definitive story of how the Wall
went up. Hard to find, but worth searching for.
Fatherland by Robert Harris. What if the Nazis won? This alternative
detective story set in 1964 post-war Berlin examines that dark scenario.
Mr Norris Changes Trains and *Goodbye to Berlin* by Christopher Isherwood.
These two works formed the basis for a stage play *I am a Camera*
and the more famous musical and movie *Cabaret*. The stories provide
a vivid description of life in the city in the early days of Nazism.
Stasiland by Anna Funder. Documents the effects of the Stasi on the
lives of East Berliners.

Emergencies

The following are emergency numbers:
Ambulance 🕿 112
Fire brigade 🕿 112
Police 🕿 110

MEDICAL SERVICES
Medical treatment in Germany is of a high standard but expensive.
EU residents should carry a European Health Insurance Card (EHIC) and
all travellers are advised to take out comprehensive travel insurance.

Pharmacies (*Apotheken*)
Pharmacies in Germany are denoted by a large, stylised 'A' on a white
background. While most pharmacies are closed on Sunday and from
around midday on Saturday, the **Apotheke Berlin Hauptbahnhof**
(🖂 Europaplatz 1, Berlin Hauptbahnhof 🕿 (030) 2061 4190) is open
24 hours, seven days per week. You'll find it in Berlin's main train station.

Hospitals
Charité Campus Mitte 🖂 Chariteplatz 1 🕿 (030) 450 531 000
🌐 www.charite.de
Vivantes Klinikum Am Urban (Kreuzberg) 🖂 Dieffenbachstrasse 1
🕿 (030) 130 210 🌐 www.vivantes.de Ⓝ U-Bahn: Prinzenstrasse

POLICE
To contact the police in a non-emergency situation, call
🕿 (030) 4664 4664.
Charlottenburg police station 🖂 Bismarckstrasse 111
🕿 (030) 4664 2277 00

EMERGENCY PHRASES

Help!	Fire!	Stop!
Hilfe!	Feuer!	Halt!
Heelfe!	*Foyer!*	*Halt!*

Call an ambulance/a doctor/the police/the fire service!
Rufen Sie bitte einen Krankenwagen/einen Arzt/die Polizei/
die Feuerwehr!
*Roofen zee bitter inen krankenvaagen/inen artst/dee politsye/
dee foyervair!*

Kreuzberg police station ⓐ Friesenstrasse 16 ☏ (030) 46640
Mitte police station ⓐ Keibelstrasse 35 ☏ (030) 4664 3327 00
Schöneberg police station ⓐ Hauptstrasse 45 ☏ (030) 4664 4427 01

EMBASSIES & CONSULATES

Australian Embassy ⓐ Wallstrasse 76–79 ☏ (030) 880 0880
ⓦ www.germany.embassy.gov.au
British Embassy ⓐ Wilhelmstrasse 70 ☏ (030) 204 570
ⓦ http://ukingermany.fco.gov.uk
Canadian Embassy ⓐ Leipziger Platz 17 ☏ (030) 203 120
ⓦ http://germany.gc.ca
New Zealand Embassy ⓐ Friedrichstrasse 60 ☏ (030) 206 210
ⓦ www.nzembassy.com/germany
Republic of Ireland Embassy ⓐ Jägerstrasse 51 ☏ 030 220 720
ⓦ www.embassyofireland.de
US Embassy ⓐ Pariser Platz 2 ☏ (030) 83050
ⓦ http://germany.usembassy.gov

Editorial/project management: Lisa Plumridge
Copy editor: Monica Guy
Layout/DTP: Alison Rayner

The publishers would like to thank the following individuals and
organisations for supplying their copyright photographs for this book:
Paolo Bassetti, pages 29 & 66; Dainis Derics/123RF.com, page 31;
Dreamstime.com (Zaharescu Mihaela Catalina, page 22; Eugene
Gordin, page 21; Jerz, page 5; Philip Lange, pages 40–1; Nadine Lind,
page 9); Internationale Filmfestspiele Berlin/Andreas Teich, page 13;
SXC.hu (fumu, page 57; Ronny Teufert, page 33); Marcel Urech, page 17;
Christopher Holt, all others.

Send your thoughts to
books@thomascook.com

- Found a great bar, club, shop or must-see sight that we don't feature?
- Like to tip us off about any information that needs a little updating?
- Want to tell us what you love about this handy little guidebook and
  more importantly how we can make it even handier?

Then here's your chance to tell all! Send us ideas, discoveries and
recommendations today and then look out for your valuable input
in the next edition of this title.

Email the above address (stating the title) or write to:
pocket guides Series Editor, Thomas Cook Publishing, PO Box 227,
Coningsby Road, Peterborough PE3 8SB, UK.

WHAT'S IN YOUR GUIDEBOOK?

Independent authors Impartial up-to-date information from our travel experts who meticulously source local knowledge.

Experience Thomas Cook's 165 years in the travel industry and guidebook publishing enriches every word with expertise you can trust.

Travel know-how Thomas Cook has thousands of staff working around the globe, all living and breathing travel.

Editors Travel-publishing professionals, pulling everything together to craft a perfect blend of words, pictures, maps and design.

You, the traveller We deliver a practical, no-nonsense approach to information, geared to how you really use it.

Useful phrases

English	German	Approx pronunciation
BASICS		
Yes	Ja	*Yah*
No	Nein	*Nine*
Please	Bitte	*Bitter*
Thank you	Danke	*Danker*
Hello	Hallo	*Hallo*
Goodbye	Auf Wiedersehen	*Owf veederzeyhen*
Excuse me	Entschuldigen Sie	*Entshuldigen zee*
Sorry	Entschuldigung	*Entshuldigoong*
That's okay	Das stimmt	*Das shtimt*
To	Nach	*Nakh*
From	Von	*Fon*
I don't speak German	Ich spreche kein Deutsch	*Ikh shprekher kine doitsh*
Do you speak English?	Sprechen Sie Englisch?	*Shprekhen zee eng-lish?*
Good morning	Guten Morgen	*Gooten morgen*
Good afternoon	Guten Tag	*Gooten tag*
Good evening	Guten Abend	*Gooten abend*
Goodnight	Gute Nacht	*Gute nacht*
My name is ...	Mein Name ist ...	*Mine naamer ist ...*
NUMBERS		
One	Eins	*Ines*
Two	Zwei	*Tsvy*
Three	Drei	*Dry*
Four	Vier	*Feer*
Five	Fünf	*Foonf*
Six	Sechs	*Zex*
Seven	Sieben	*Zeeben*
Eight	Acht	*Akht*
Nine	Neun	*Noyn*
Ten	Zehn	*Tseyn*
Twenty	Zwanzig	*Tvantsikh*
Fifty	Fünfzig	*Foonftsikh*
One hundred	Hundert	*Hoondert*
SIGNS & NOTICES		
Airport	Flughafen	*Floogharfen*
Rail station/Platform	Bahnhof/Bahnsteig	*Baanhof/Baanshtykh*
Smoking/Non-smoking	Raucher/Nichtraucher	*Raukher/Nikhtraukher*
Toilets	Toiletten	*Toletten*
Ladies/Gentlemen	Damen/Herren	*Daamen/Herren*
Subway	Die U-Bahn	*Dee Oo-baan*